MARGAUX

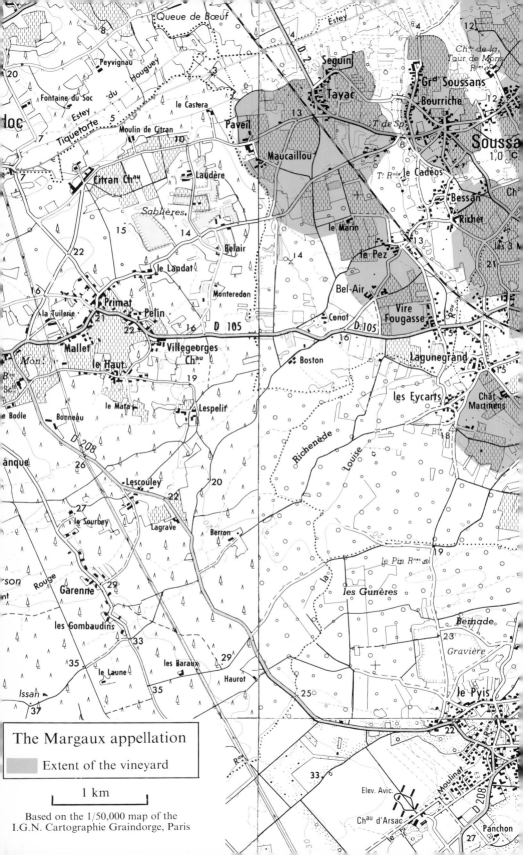

The Margaux appellation

Extent of the vineyard

1 km

Based on the 1/50,000 map of the
I.G.N. Cartographie Graindorge, Paris

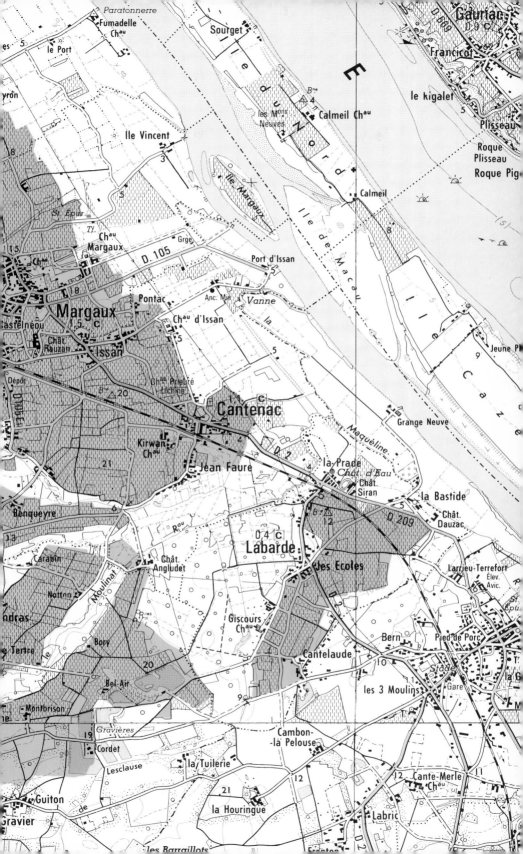

SAINT-ESTEPHE

PAUILLAC

HAUT-MEDOC

COTES DE BOURG

SAINT-JULIEN

MOULIS
LISTRAC

POM

MARGAUX

HAUT-MEDOC

GRAVES

-EMILION

THE WINES OF FRANCE

MARGAUX

Bernard Ginestet

Foreword by Hugh Johnson

Holt, Rinehart and Winston
New York

Copyright © 1984 by Jacques Legrand SA
English translation Copyright © 1985 by D. Healey
Foreword Copyright © 1985 by Hugh Johnson

First published in the United States in January 1986 by
Holt, Rinehart and Winston, 383 Madison Avenue,
New York, New York 10017.

Published simultaneously in Canada by Holt, Rinehart and Winston of Canada, Limited.

Originally published in France under the title *Margaux* by Librairie Fernand Nathan.

Library of Congress Cataloging-in-Publication Data

Ginestet, Bernard.
    The wines of France. Margaux.

    Translation of: Margaux.
    1. Wine and wine making — France — Margaux.   I. Title.
TP553.G56713 1985   641.2'22'094471   85–17712
ISBN 0–03–006014–1

First American Edition

Designer: Henri Marganne

Printed in Holland

10 9 8 7 6 5 4 3 2 1

ISBN 0-03-006014-1

Contents

Foreword by Hugh Johnson   13

The Story of the Margaux Appellation   17

The *Crus*   95

    Château d'Angludet   97
    Château Baudry   98
    Château Bel Air-Marquis d'Aligre   99
    Château Bellegarde   100
    Clos de Bigos   101
    Château Bory   101
    Bouquet de Monbrison   101
    Château Boyd-Cantenac   101
    Château Brane-Cantenac   103
    Château Cantenac Brown   105
    Château Canuet   106
    Château des Carabins   106
    Cru de Castelbruck   107
    Château Charmant   108
    Château Clairefont   108
    Château Clos de La Gravière   108
    Domaine de Cure-Bourse   109
    Château Dauzac   109
    Château Desmirail   111
    Château Deyrem-Valentin   112
    Château Dupeyron   112
    Château Durfort-Vivens   112
    Château Ferrière   114
    Domaine de Fontarney   115
    Château Gassies du Vieux-Bourg   115
    Château Giscours   115
    Château Graveline   118
    Château Gravières de Marsac   118
    Château des Graviers   118
    Château Haut Breton Larigaudière   119
    Château Hautes Graves   120
    Château Haut-Tayac   120
    Château d'Issan   121
    Château Kirwan   124

Château Labégorce	126
Château Labégorce Zédé	128
Château Labory de Tayac	129
Château La Coste	129
Château La Galiane	129
Château La Gombeaude	130
Château La Gurgue	130
Clos de L'Aiguillette	131
Château de L'Amiral	131
Domaine La Rose Maucaillou	131
Château Larruau	132
Château Lascombes	133
Château La Tour de Bessan	135
Château La Tour-de-Mons	136
Clos de La Tourelle	137
Château Les Baraillots	137
Château Les Graves du Sol	138
Château Les Gravières	138
Château Ligondras	138
Château Loyac	138
Château Malescot Saint-Exupéry	139
Château Margaux	141
Château Marquis d'Alesme-Becker	148
Château Marquis de Terme	150
Château Marsac Séguineau	152
Château Martinens	153
Domaine de Maucaillou	155
Château Monbrison	155
Enclos de Moncabon	157
Château Mongravey	157
Château Montbrun	157
Château Notton	158
Château Palmer	158
Château Paveil de Luze	162
Pavillon Blanc du Château Margaux	163
Pavillon Rouge du Château Margaux	164
Château de Pichecan	164
Château Pontac-Lynch	164
Château Pontet-Chappaz	166
Château Pouget	166
Château Prieuré-Lichine	167

Clos des Quatre Vents   169
Château Rambaud   170
Château Rausan-Ségla   171
Château Rauzan-Gassies   173
Saint-Jacques   174
Château Saint-Marc   175
Château Siran   175
Château Tayac   179
Château Tayac-Plaisance   180
Château du Tertre   180
Domaine des Treilles   181
Château des Trois Chardons   182
Château Vallière   182
Cru du Vieux Cep   183
Château Vincent   184

Appendices   185

Measurements
1 hectare = 10,000 square metres = 2.471 acres
1 are = 100 square metres = 119.6 square yards

1 kilometre = 0.6214 mile (5/8 mile)
1 metre = 39.37 inches

1 *tonneau* = 9 hectolitres
1 hectolitre = 100 litres = 22 gallons (26.5 US gallons)
1 litre = 1.76 pints or 0.22 gallon (0.265 US gallon)

1 *journal* = 'the area of vines that can be worked by one
             man in a day'

Foreword

The range and focus of the discussion of wine over the last ten years or so has been like a zoom lens dissolving a crowd scene to pick on a granule of the big picture. From the days when Lichine's *The Wines of France* was considered a pretty specialized book, publishers moved, not at all long ago, to regional volumes on Bordeaux, Burgundy and the other famous vineyards. With this series wine-scholarship takes the logical next step: it focuses on the commune as the unit, at the same time narrowing the focus and allowing us a far greater insight into its components, its methods and motives.

There is a more microscopic view still: that of the individual property. *Premiers crus* and other lordly estates with long histories are suitable subjects for such treatment, but not on the whole the wine-growing property of the middle to upper rank, whose historical peculiarities are less important than their present-day make-up and morale. For them it seems eminently appropriate to take the communal view: close enough to enjoy the detail, but distant enough to make useful comparisons.

This series differs in another, perhaps even more important way from the great majority of books about wine. Most authors review the subject from the standpoint of a more or less disinterested observer and consumer. This makes them strong on comparison – at any rate superficially – but often weak on insight. Bernard Ginestet is an author who addresses the world from the very heart of his theme. He is a passionately involved insider in Bordeaux, a man who has made a score of vintages, has dealt in the biggest stakes in the business as proprietor of Château Margaux, has participated in the manoeuvres of the market as a *négociant*. A man not to be fooled: enthusiastic, yes, but not starry-eyed. Steeped as he is in the region, he cannot hide his feelings for long. Sometimes they are written on the lines, sometimes between them. Always, even behind some seemingly bland report, you feel the beat of the author's pulse.

Facts and statistics are the bare bones of the books. No detail of *encépagement*, of vinification, of production or availability or soil; no label, no telephone number even is omitted. The flesh on these bones is history, anecdote, and above all experience.

The story starts with the physical and historical groundwork, including new geological maps in fascinating detail. The heart of the introduction is the gastronomic question – what is the identity of this appellation? How do you recognize its wines? How do its citizens view them, use them, and marry them with local ingredients in local dishes?

The repertoire of châteaux follows, leaving nothing out: a piece of research of inestimable value that goes far beyond any other document I know in its scope, even leaving aside the author's deep involvement with his subject. It does not attempt to be particular about wines and vintages. This is not a book of tasting notes – rather the book that enables you to taste with discrimination; to know what it is you are tasting and to draw accurate conclusions. The single consistent conclusion that the author draws is the *rapport qualité-prix*, or value-for-money, indicated by a row of glasses. The more full glasses, the higher his rating.

The photographs, specially commissioned for the series, do not need my encomiums. I need only say that each volume can teach you more about each commune than would a dozen visits without such a guide.

Hugh Johnson

Versons ces roses près ce vin
Près ce vin versons ces roses!
Et buvons l'un à l'autre, afin
Qu'au coeur nos tristesses encloses
Prennent en buvant quelque fin.

Ronsard

The Story of the
Margaux Appellation

If the idea of sampling a selection of Margaux wines without paying through the nose appeals to you, try making friends with a fireman. The Margaux firemen's feast-day, that of Sainte-Barbe, is traditionally celebrated on the first or second Sunday of December. Three of the twenty-one man strong fire service are 'volunteered' to provide the wine. The celebrations include a high mass, a procession to the town monument where wreaths are placed, and a performance by the local jazz band, 'Prestige Margaux'. The band is conducted by the young Pascal Nouaux, whose parents are vineyard owners at Château Margaux. After the presentation of certificates of honour and medals, the congratulatory speeches by the head of the fire brigade and the mayor, the deputy – if he is there – says his few words, and the local councillor adds his own; after the toast and the lengthy procedure of seating all the guests, the banquet can at last begin.

The firemen usually manage, during their training courses, to visit the local *chais*. Each owner puts aside a small case of wine for them and the wine cellar of the CPI (Centre de première intervention) in Margaux is one of the best in the whole commune. The menu is usually more than adequate and might include:

Soupe de poissons
Huîtres et crépinettes
Ragoût de sanglier
Pintade flambée au cognac
Pommes dauphines
Haricots verts au jus
Salade de saison
Plateau de fromages
Forêt Noire

Vins de Margaux

Café-Liqueurs

The wines follow, one after the other, for a good five hours, usually from one in the afternoon until six. They are sniffed, admired, tasted and criticized. The different vintages are compared and evaluated. Everyone reminisces about what they were doing that year: 'You remember, the year that there was that fire at Joseph's ... Yes, it was terribly cold at the start of May in 1974 ... There was that dreadful pale red moon that brought on the terrible frosts every morning for at least five days – especially near Virefougasse ... Yes, but Virefougasse isn't even the Margaux appellation area ... Really? Are you sure? ... Yes it's true ... Sometimes it does well ... Ah yes, but only in the good years ... And then of course, it's really in Soussans. That's not really anything to do with Margaux ... Just a minute, taste this Marquis de Terme ... I find it much more subtle than the Lascombes ... That's because it's much older ... That's the trick, my friend, the ageing ... Well actually, I almost prefer the Larruau ... Yes, that's the wine that little château makes, isn't it? ... Bernard Château ... Yes, it's odd being called 'château' in Margaux! ... Well, yes, but he certainly makes some good wine ... It really is tremendously good ... Taste it ... Then afterwards we can try the Rauzan-Gassies ... Hey, Francis! Pass the Rauzan-Gassies ... Well, we certainly had some fine crops this year, that's for sure ... Yes, it's true. It really was a bumper harvest ... Wasn't it, Father?'

The parish of Margaux is a flat area, lying on the left bank of the Gironde, with the church only an eighth of a league away. The soil in Margaux is of the finest gravelly type, and as a result some very fine, well-known wines are made there. The ones produced by Château Margaux itself are so well known that they have been sold for up to a hundred Louis a *tonneaux*. The land around the parish bordering on the river is divided into fine meadows which stretch out for a considerable distance beyond the town. The main product of Margaux is wine.

The parish is bordered to the east by the Gironde and to the west partly by the parish of Soussans, partly by Cantenac; the latter also expands to the south, and Soussans marks the northern extremity of Margaux. The town is five leagues from Bordeaux and about two from Castlenau. There is a small post office, which deals with all the local mail except on Sundays. The parish is about two leagues wide; the village known as Doumench, which is the furthest from the church, is no more than a quarter of a league away. The main road, which runs from Bordeaux to Pauliac, and then on to the Bas-Médoc, crosses Margaux from south to north.

There are two ports in Margaux, one being the Port du Roi, and the other which bears the name of the parish. The latter belongs to the Lord of Margaux and is now almost completely disused, being totally silted up, and the other is well on the way to being in the same state because of the sandbanks which have formed in front of it, rendering access extremely difficult. Before the sandbanks were there, both ports were extremely busy and there was some small amount of trade in corn and flour within the parish and the surrounding area. But the main occupation of the local people is indisputably wine-making.

Thank God there has always been a priest in Margaux! Since this passage was written, in 1784, by the Abbé Baurein in his *Variétés bordelaises*, the port of Margaux has had no further involvement in the corn and flour trade. The main occupation of the inhabitants, however, is still wine-making – and making sure that the wines produced today are as good as they were in the eighteenth century.

It was during the years 1720–30 that the Margaux vineyard first became famous. Grapes had been grown there since the late Middle Ages, but the idea of a *grand cru* was almost unknown and the wine trade was extremely unstable. This was the case practically all over the Bordeaux region, and certainly applied to the Médoc, where with rare exceptions the 'châteaux' moved into full wine production only after the reign of Louis XIV. Prior to that a few of the local lords, rich landowners, had divided up the wine production of the area between them and the vineyards were leased to the local peasants.

In this way each wine-producing family was responsible for a handful of strips of land which were measured in '*journaux*'. These were described as the area that one man was capable of working in a day. The harvests were then made individually and the wine was pressed straight into the '*tonneaux*' which held about 9 hectolitres, serving as containers for both ageing and transporting the wine. (The *tonneau* is a practical measure still used throughout the Bordeaux area. It is roughly equivalent to four barrels of 225 litres which should produce some 300 0.75cl bottles each. Usually this figure is reduced by various losses and other occurrences to the region of 1152 bottles to a *tonneau*. More and more often nowadays the *grands crus* are sold by the case of twelve bottles.)

The wines therefore varied greatly from one producer to the next. They were normally grouped together under the name of the parish in which they were produced – thus one could distinguish between the wines of Cantenac and those of Margaux. There was, however, a kind of family resemblance between the wines from a particular area that the shippers were quick to name the 'type'. In his fine book, *Le Goût du vin*, Professor Emile Peynaud puts forward the theory that this 'type' was purely and simply a fabrication which was extremely advantageous to the shippers. In this case, my own humble opinion is rather less definite. Even if this idea of a manufactured 'type' is true – since

the idea was well accepted, particularly by the professional Bordeaux wine-producers – there is real evidence to suggest that the wine from a particular area does in fact have its own characteristic traits. I will come back to this argument later.

Up to the end of the seventeenth century there was in Margaux, as in Sauternes, Pomerol, Pommard, and Rivesaltes, a large quantity of fine wines. Making the choice from such a varied selection was very difficult, and to make it easier courtiers were sent out into the country to fetch back samples to the larger wine companies in Bordeaux. The terms and conditions of each deal, indeed of each *tonneau* supplied, were extremely demanding in a way that we, with the advantage of the telephone and telex machines, cannot now easily appreciate.

The noble families of the *ancien régime* knew what they were about. However much we may dispute the matter, blue blood was certainly

Just before entering the village of Margaux, on the road from Bordeaux, one can see on the right the parish church which was formerly the private chapel of Château La Mothe, former name of Château Margaux. To the left is Château Abel-Laurent.

able to appreciate reds and whites. Recognizing the potential of the wine-growing industry, the noblemen were quick to bestow their family names on the wines produced on their estates. They began by printing their coats of arms on the casks, and later on the labels themselves. These marquis, counts, viscounts and barons were well known in the Louvre and in the Parliament at Bordeaux, including among them such names as Bel-Air, Marquis d'Aligre, Marquis de Terme, Durfort and Comte de Vivens. This noble list was increased each century by such people as the Barons de Rothschild at Paulliac, the Comte de Saint-Exupéry and the Baron de Brane at Margaux. Their modern-day counterpart, Alexis Lichine, is now the well known proprietor of Château Prieuré-Lichine.

Between them, the shippers and the noble families introduced the idea of specific *crus*. I would like to emphasize the cooperation that went into this task, which today is somewhat overlooked. The nobility were in no way renowned for their ability to sell their own products. On the other hand, they were a wonderful source of publicity and public relations well before the appearance of *Vogue* magazine. They were encouraged by the shippers to recognize the economic viability

of commercial wine production and to refine this production, making only thoroughbred wines.

It was against this backdrop of commercial rivalry that the 'second Hundred Years War' was waged between 1750 and 1850. It could also be called the 'War of the Châteaux', since the owners, holidaying on their lands once or twice a year, usually at harvest time, were determined to announce their prosperity, however precarious, to all the world. This developed into a real mania for grandiose building projects. Some built upwards, measuring their status against the height of the keeps, bell towers and turrets they built. Others, with a rather better appreciation of the situation, built an endless succession of halls, entrance rooms and corridors leading to numerous reception rooms. Some of the wealthy spent their passion for construction producing magnificent façades. This building programme produced a quantity of magnificent mansions in which may be found the imposing works of both neo-Gothic and Renaissance architects. At the same time, the vineyards were reorganized, the *chais* were enlarged or reconstructed, and the vat houses were equipped with up-to-date presses, tanning drums and large fermenting vats.

It was at this time that the modern idea of wine production first took shape. In fact, as far as the older kind of château is concerned, there is only one example within the Margaux appellation predating the seventeenth century, that being the Château d'Issan in the Cantenac commune. Even the use of the term 'château' to distinguish the place of production of a particular wine is relatively recent. In the 1855 classification only Lafite, Margaux, Latour, Issan and Beychevelle were designated 'châteaux'. The other wines were simply named after the main town in their area of production, occasionally followed by the name of the owner. (We should not forget that labelling was extremely rare at that time and was usually done by the shippers or wine-importers.)

It is easy nowadays to mock the Bordeaux predilection for the use of the term 'châteaux', whether it be in the Médoc, Sauternes, Graves or elsewhere. Some journalists are certainly not slow to criticize this snobbishness. In all fairness, however, it does serve a sound commercial purpose. 'If one wishes to be a wine-grower, one must be visible,' writes Pierre-Marie Doutrelant in his book *Les Bons Vins et les autres*: 'One must have a château, turrets and gilded china. There must be rose

◀ *This fine statue of a worshipper of Bacchus is in the garden of Château Lascombes.*

The façade of Château Margaux has been used as an illustration in all the works produced on the wines of Bordeaux since the nineteenth century. This is a little-known Italian engraving from the 3rd Empire.   ▶ 23

25

bushes among the vines, grand dinner parties, hunting and balls and a staff of at least thirty the whole year round. One must sell oneself and above all the mystique of the old aristocracy!' This explanation is somewhat misleading in that the original meaning of the word snobbery is 'lacking in nobility'. P.-M. Doutrelant forgets that the real *raison d'être* of the wine-growing nobility is their vineyards. These owners and their staff dedicate their lives to the production of a superior product. They are privileged to live in a château which was built by somebody else and is often decorated with turrets. They do not repair their roofs simply for show. And as for planting rose bushes among the vines, this is only practical because their staff prune and fertilize them as they tend the vines themselves and besides, it is a service to everybody, making the whole countryside much more attractive. Gilded china looks extremely well on white tablecloths which also bring out the colour of the wines; all these are simply family heirlooms brought out to honour invited guests. As for hunting and balls, these would appear to be more than appropriate pastimes for people who produce both good wine and good living. M. Doutrelant reminds me of R. J. Courtine* waxing lyrical before a small pot of lentils accompanied by a red Bouzy and castigating the indecent precocity of a fine Médoc wine served in a crystal decanter by the wine waiter in a well-known three-star restaurant.

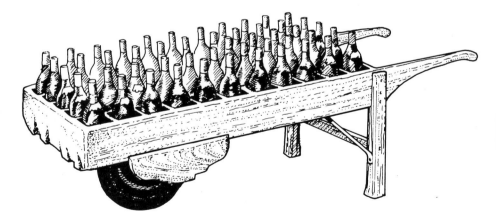

At the centre of the *grands crus* produced in the five communes of the Margaux appellation stands Château Margaux itself. The wine is peculiar in having the same name as the appellation area and although

*R.-J. Courtine produced gastronomic articles for several years in the magazine Cuisine et vins de France under the pseudonym 'Convive grincheux'.

this can sometimes be a source of confusion on wine lists there are obviously benefits to be derived from it. Since Château Margaux is well known throughout the world, the other *crus* associated with its name share its fame. The appearance of the name Margaux on the labels of the seventy-odd owners in the appellation area has also helped to publicize the name of Château Margaux itself. The communes constituting the Margaux appellation area are, from north to south, Soussans, Margaux, Arsac, Cantenac and Labarde. The Margaux postal area (33460) covers nine communes, to include Macau to the east and Arcins, Lamarque and Cussac-Fort-Médoc to the northwest. These latter are not in any way associated with the Margaux appellation, being rather 'Bordeaux' or 'Bordeaux Supérieur' or even 'Haut-Médoc' and the wines produced in these four communes are never labelled 'Margaux' except as part of their postal address. It is sometimes difficult for the layman to find his way through this tangle of local customs. To complicate matters further, inside the area of the commune 'AOC Margaux' are lands which have no right to use the appellation. These are sandy stretches lying mainly to the south of Arsac and Cantenac and some richer clayey soil, known as *palus*, beside the river. (The Domaine de l'Ile-Margaux, for example, is a small muddy islet in the Garonne, straddling the communes of Cantenac and Margaux; but it produces nothing more than good Bordeaux supérieur.) The title normally used is:

Margaux
Appellation d'Origine Contrôlée

or sometimes:

Appellation Margaux Contrôlée

These – to all intents and purposes the same – are extremely precise and the best evidence that the wine is in fact a true Margaux. This helps to avoid any confusion by the over-use of the Margaux name, whether it be on wine labels or in advertising, on headed writing paper or shipping invoices.

The AOC Margaux was finally introduced by law on 10 August 1954. This was well after the other well-known Médoc appellations but it was certainly well worth waiting for. The process had taken some fifty years, during which the Margaux wine-producers and those of the surrounding area waged a fierce battle.

Directly facing Château Rausan-Ségla is one of the best examples of the typical Margaux gravelly vineyards. ▶

Well before this contemporary struggle, the parishes of Margaux and Soussans were at daggers drawn. Back in the fifteenth and sixteenth centuries the priests of Saint-Michel de Margaux and Saint-Romain de Soussans were accustomed to encouraging their flocks into battle, sometimes even bringing black magic into use for their cause. At dead of night, they would release black hens into the neighbouring vineyards to contaminate the coming harvest. During the Rogations, this holy war sometimes took a rather more physical turn. The processions began early each morning, covering the whole of the parish. They would stop before the altars of repose in front of the various farms and at each signpost marking the crossroads of the country lanes. On tables covered with embroidered cloths, flowers and divine images, they would set out offerings to God, asking for his blessing on the assembled company and the forthcoming harvest. The whole procession was followed by a cart loaded with food for the worshippers. One of the country lanes was ripe for incident in that it was the dividing line between the two parishes. Several scuffles took place there over the centuries and, in 1592, three days before the feast of the Ascension, the vying processions of Soussans and Margaux found themselves face to face on this road. There was certainly no question of either of them giving ground to the other and the narrowness of the lane made it impossible for them to pass in peace. They began by shouting and waving banners and crosses at each other. Then the altar boys, in a fit of patriotic fervour, exchanged blows with their opposite numbers. The patronesses of the opposing camps belaboured each other with hymn books, and the sacristans, urged on by their respective priests, fought a duel with holy-water sprinklers. The priests themselves chose to raise the tone of the whole proceedings by cursing each other in Latin. By the end of that day, both in Margaux and Soussans, there was many a bruised forehead and many a stained garment. From that moment on, no love was lost between the two villages and this rivalry is still well remembered today.

Since the turn of the century, there has been a series of law suits between the wine-growers of Margaux and Soussans, the former being determined to prevent the latter using the name of Margaux on their wines. Things were further complicated in that several of the Margaux *grands crus classés* have property in Soussans. How then, could it be

---

In the commune of Soussans, beside the stream of La Louise, the tower of Bessan stands as a reminder of the wars previously fought on Médoc soil when it was the English who harvested the area. ▶

Vats of freshly picked grapes arriving at the Château d'Angludet. They are transported by rail
to the outhouses where the vinification process begins. ▶ ▶

possible for them to deny the use of an appellation to property which produced the same wine as their own? The Margaux Owners Association, founded in 1923, took as its main objective the protection and defence of the Margaux name. After a long series of court battles, the association managed to obtain a declaration that the wines of the Soussans commune were no longer entitled to use the Margaux appellation, and that this was a final judgement and any new evidence brought forward to reopen the case should be deemed inadmissible. As for the owners with property in Soussans, it was stated that it was one thing for them to have the right of use of the appellation and another for it to be granted to owners situated in the neighbouring communes which had nothing at all to do with Margaux. This fierce battle was intensified by the pretensions of the widow Domenech de Celles who, at the beginning of the century, took it upon herself to name her produce '*vin de Margaux*' although it was in fact from the Ile de Fumadelle, on the very furthest boundary of the Soussans commune. There was also a M. Clauzel, a producer at Avensan, who was taken to court for misuse of the Margaux name. In 1919, there was a whole group of communes wishing, without renouncing their own identity, to label their wines Margaux. These included not only the present-day users of the appellation, but also Arcins, Avensan, Listrac, Moulis and Le Pian. This was certainly taking things a little too far.

The conflict finally came to a head in true Clochemerle fashion, worthy of the previous battles fought hand-to-hand on the roads of Margaux. The Braquessac family, living in Margaux, had only their *chais* and 3000 *pieds* of vines on 80 acres of property within the commune, while they had 3 hectares at Soussans, 1 at Cantenac and 30,000 *pieds* elsewhere. In short, they were in name owners in Margaux but their authentic *vin de Margaux* was no more than a drop in the ocean compared to their total production. The Braquessac family became, against their will, the scapegoat of the most distinguished lawyers in Bordeaux. Local politics became involved and the municipal councillor of Margaux added his support to M. Braquessac. This did not prevent them, however, from being judged guilty at their appeal and being demoted.

To cut a long story short, it was finally the *crus classés* around Margaux which redeemed the appellation. Their property covered the communes of Margaux, Arsac, Cantenac, Labarde and Soussans. None of the major landowners were really interested in destroying the functional entity of the appellation, as that would have resulted in a lot of scattered parcels of land. Desmirail, Marquis de Terme, Giscours, Cantenac-Brown and several of the *crus bourgeois supérieurs* had large properties in Arsac and although there is no *cru classé* named in Soussans, the majority of the Margaux *crus classés* own land there. Even Château Margaux itself has important vineyards in Cantenac and Soussans.

Five years before the official classification of 1855, Charles Cocks published, through Féret et Fils in Bordeaux, his *Guide de l'étranger à Bordeaux et dans la Gironde: Bordeaux, ses environs et ses vins, classés par ordre de mérite.* (This book is the direct ancestor of the whole collection of the *Bordeaux et ses vins* series commonly known as 'Le Féret'.) Cocks had these comments to make on each of the five communes in question.

Arsac: This area has extremely pebbly soil and produces wines which are full-bodied and well-rounded. They have a fine colour and bouquet; they are similar to the wines produced in Cantenac and Margaux and should be bottled after five years.

Cantenac: The soil here is pebbly, black and white and sandy. The wines are strong and have such good qualities that they rival those of the best Médoc communes. They have a fine bouquet and mellow texture which, along with their fine colour and full body, is particularly distinctive.

Labarde: This tiny commune is in an extremely picturesque setting. Wine is the only crop grown here, and the soil, both gravelly and sandy, produces wines superior to that of Macau, extremely agreeable to the palate and with a fine colour and bouquet.

Margaux: This area produces the best-known wines in the region. These wines, according to their maturity, are endowed with finesse, good colour and a fine bouquet. They are full-bodied without being heady, they are gentle on the stomach and the head, and leave the breath fresh and the mouth clean. Their reputation has spread throughout Europe.

Soussans: Although this commune is extremely close to Margaux, its wine does not enjoy the same reputation, although the best growths of the Margaux commune, most notably that of Château Margaux, own large areas of vines within Soussans. The wines are strong, and rich in vigour and colour. They are, however, a little hard and only at their best after six years or so.

These comments, while remaining close to those made by William Franck in his first *Treatise on the Wines of the Médoc* written in 1824, make a fine distinction between the respective qualities of the five communes without being too harsh on any of them. They attempt to define the 'types' of each area taken as a communal entity. This is really where the shoe pinches, since however well-meaning such a generalization may be, the law which has declared where the boundaries of an appellation should be drawn has been linked too closely to that of the commune layout and not closely enough to the real distinguishing features of the geology, climate and agricultural characteristics of the area. It is necessary to define the use of an appellation (Margaux or not Margaux, that is the question), and where a wine like Château Margaux has a reputation which is the envy of all its neighbours, there will always be dispute. The wines in the appellations of Saint-Julien, Paulliac and Saint-Estèphe, to name but a few, are much easier to define than those entitled to the Margaux name because there is no confusion between the châteaux wine itself and the produce of the whole commune. If Lafite, Latour and Haut-Brion were parish names, all the local parishes and those in the surrounding area would have wanted to take on the same name. (It is remarkable that throughout the Gironde wherever there is a commonplace village such as Lafite or Latour, the owner is quick to inscribe this on his wine labels and sell his produce at a higher price than his neighbours. As for Mouton-Rothschild, it has produced a test-tube baby known as Mouton-Cadet.)

The problem of the postal address is distinct, as we have seen, from that of the appellation, but nevertheless is irrevocably bound with 'local usage, loyalty and constancy'. The same problem was faced, but in a different fashion, during the building of the railroads throughout France and the Médoc. Nowadays, Margaux station is only a small stop on the line from Bordeaux to Pointe de Grave owned by the 'Chemins de fer économiques du Médoc', a lowly but costly subsidiary

of the SNCF. Formerly, however, when steam trains were the main means of communication and commerce, the situation was very different. Every Friday evening Margaux station was full of rich Bordeaux families arriving to spend the weekend at their country properties. They were met by various members of their household staff amid a confusion of voices, bells, stamping horses and cracking whips. A whole generation which was familiar with such sights at the turn of the century has now disappeared. In my childhood these scenes were vividly described to me. At the time, the *tonneaux* were also transported by rail as a means of replacing the previous shipping traffic, since the ports of Issan, Margaux and Soussans were increasingly unusable because of silt deposit.

The commune of Cantenac had no station of its own and, as a result, Margaux became the centre of transport for both communes. It was at this point that the mayor of Cantenac called for the name of Margaux station to be changed to Margaux-Cantenac. On 28 August 1892 there was a heated exchange between the various parties and the mayor's proposition was overruled by nine votes to three. In May 1896 at the municipal elections, both mayors and the councillors were replaced and the Cantenac commune once more called for the name change. A committee was set up to study the proposal, and on 23 May 1897 the Margaux municipal council reaffirmed the previous ruling, qualifying its decision as follows:

> Taking into account that it is not a simple whim on the part of the Cantenac commune to wish to associate its name with that of the Margaux commune, but rather that it is in the hope of profiting by this association, it is sufficient to repeat the ruling of August 1892, in which, by a large majority, the council declared its opposition to such an association;
>
> Taking into account that the reason for this demand is obviously to enable the celebrated wine-producing commune of Cantenac to enjoy the even greater reputation of that of Margaux. This worldwide fame has facilitated the sale of Margaux wines and has increased profits from such sales; it is hardly surprising that many producers of more mediocre products throughout the world, even in California, have expressed a wish to associate their names with Margaux. It is, therefore, no less surprising that the wine-producers of Cantenac should seek to profit from the union of the names of Margaux and Cantenac;
>
> Taking into account that while such a union might be extremely profitable for the wine-growers of Cantenac, it can in no way enhance the reputation of the Margaux commune;

Taking into account that if the Cantenac commune is displeased that its name does not appear either on the railway schedules or on the signs on the Médoc line, it would be far more logical for them to ask for their name to be joined to that of the station nearest to them; which, in this case, is that of Labarde, since Cantenac is one kilometre from there while, even by the most direct route, it is three from Margaux;

Taking into account that the Cantenac commune is well aware of the scandalous abuse already made of the name of Margaux, they can in no way expect that such abuse could, in any way, be sanctioned officially by the artificial linking of the name of Cantenac to that of Margaux;

Taking into account that the name of the Margaux commune is, in its way, as respected as that of a great family and that any abuse of such a name could lead to the destruction of the reputation with

There are many other businesses which flourish as a result of the wine-making industry. In Margaux, Robert Bergey makes the traditional cases which hold 12 bottles each of the grand cru.

a consequential loss of revenue and commercial value to Margaux and the wine-growing community in general, any kind of joint identity could only result in damage to the good name and value of the Margaux properties;

Finally, taking into account that should such a precedent be set, there would be no good reason for refusing similar demands introduced by the communes of Arsac and Soussans which, in turn, could lead to the establishment of an association of names such as Margaux-Cantenac-Soussans-Arsac, which obviously would do nothing to enhance the reputation of any of the parties concerned . . .

I shall not comment further on the general nature of the document as it first appeared, but it is obvious that it sums up the greater part of the argument put forward during the proceedings for the establishment of the Margaux appellation, which lasted for more than fifty years. The ruling was given to include the previously mentioned five communes. It is impossible to deny the part played by the Médoc railways in the unification of Margaux, but the station remains known simply as Margaux and its goods-train shed is nowadays rented by a wine-case maker who uses it as a warehouse, prior to delivery to the great châteaux. Nowdays the wine is transported by truck along the very route which was previously the scene of inter-communal battles!

An official from the Institut National des Appellations d'Origine (INAO), M. Laffourgue, produced a detailed report in 1942. It acknowledged the rights of Cantenac and Soussans to be placed within the Margaux appellation, at the same time excluding Arsac and Labarde from this judgement. Although Soussans was admitted to have a good case, the previous judgement was adhered to and finally the commune was not admitted. Once again, the Margaux owners with property in Soussans were deprived of the largest part of their Margaux wine production.

There followed ten troubled years at the end of which the INAO changed its mind: Soussans remained excluded but Cantenac, Arsac and Labarde were admitted. Paul Zuger, who was at the time president of the Association of Margaux Owners for the Protection and Defence of the Name of Margaux, was himself owner of a large amount of land at Marsac in Soussans. It was one of the best areas in the country, where many *grands crus*, including Château Margaux, had property. M. Zuger was moved to write to the director of the INAO as follows: 'It seems to me scandalous and senseless to grant the rights to Margaux appellation to properties which are 6 or 7 kilometres from Margaux, while the neighbouring vineyard of

Soussans-Marsac is judged unworthy. This cannot, in all conscience, be allowed to continue, for the judgements made seem to be inexplicable, ill-conceived, old-fashioned and absurd.'

Another powerful argument was added to this when the Bordeaux shippers let it be known that in order for Margaux to be viable for commercial exploitation as an appellation, it was absolutely necessary that there should be enough produce for wide distribution, and this was impossible without using all the natural resources from the Margaux region.

This resulted, as we have seen, in the decision of 10 August 1954.

On 20 January 1683 Jean-Baptiste Colbert, the King's minister and adviser, wrote to his intendant in Bordeaux: 'These merchants seem to know more than the magistrates.'

Being a merchant involves not only knowing how to sell, but also knowing what to buy. With regard to wine, this knowledge is at once both indispensable and delicate. With the majority of wine now being château-bottled and the double problem of protecting the producer and his product and also protecting the consumer through guarantees of authenticity, the merchants have become prolific telex-senders and wine-catalogue editors. They buy certain varieties and resell them.

It is really for the consumer to decide between the good and the bad wines, since these will always exist and a wine-producer will never admit that his wine is bad. A clever merchant will know how to avoid offering such wines, and will thus endorse his customers' confidence in him. But there are always people within this system who are willing to abuse it. As for Margaux, like the majority of the great Bordeaux appellations, I would affirm that it is the business houses of Bordeaux which have built, maintained and demonstrated the full glory of the wines. They were certainly aware of the solid foundation on which they built, but, nevertheless, we should credit them for their enterprise.

It is well known that the majority of wines sold in Bordeaux are not produced on *graves* and that there are a great number produced on the richer loam *palus*, which produce much thinner and harder wines so popular with people from the North. It is up to those who buy them to accept them on their own merits and not to take them, with the pompous titles bestowed on them by the merchants, at their face value. All the merchants are skilled in singing the praises of their own particular produce. These more common wines, if well chosen, travel and age well and taste far better in the islands than back in the country of their production. (*Nouveau voyage aux isles de l'Amérique, Paris, 1722*)

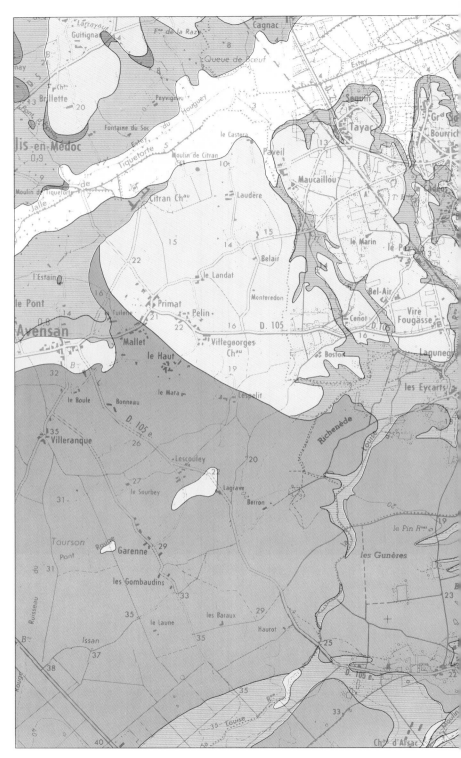

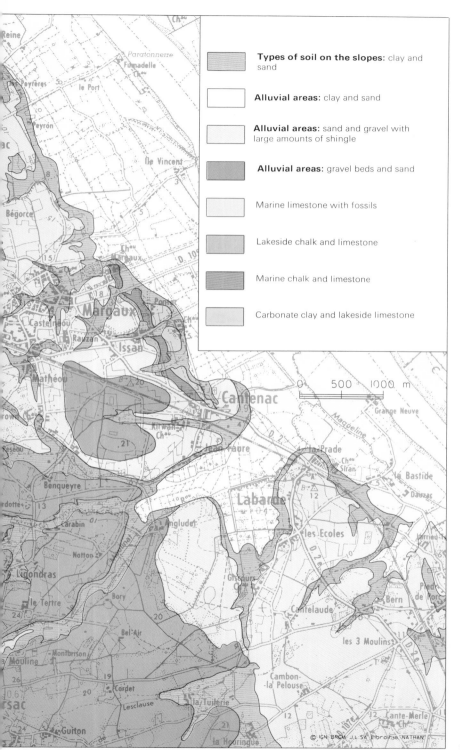

Types of soil on the slopes: clay and sand

Alluvial areas: clay and sand

Alluvial areas: sand and gravel with large amounts of shingle

Alluvial areas: gravel beds and sand

Marine limestone with fossils

Lakeside chalk and limestone

Marine chalk and limestone

Carbonate clay and lakeside limestone

0   500   1000 m

© IGN BRGM J.L SA Librairie NATHAN

43

This distinction between the wines produced on the *graves* (gravelly or clayey soil beds) and those produced on *palus* (richer alluvial soil beds) is the basis for differentiating between the Bordeaux vineyards. It is, however, essential to understand that the term '*vins de Graves*' covers all the *crus* grown on the gravelly soil terraces which principally form the modern wine-growing region of Graves, to the south-west of Bordeaux, and the whole of the Haut-Médoc as far as Saint-Estèphe. For a wine-lover in 1750, 'Graves' meant the whole of the gravelly area on the left bank of the Garonne and the Gironde. It is because of the urban sprawl of Bordeaux, which has spread out into the surrounding wine-producing areas, that this geological definition has been cut into two halves, the southern part retaining the name of 'Graves' and the northern part becoming the 'Médoc'.

In short, in the eighteenth century Margaux wine was well and truly a Graves. Further evidence for this was found in the *Mémoire sur le commerce du Bordeaux* of 1730:

There are five main *crus* in the seneschalcy of Bordeaux, these being Graves, Palu, Entre-deux-Mers, Langon, Barsac and Preignac. Each of these *crus* are subdivided, according to the different prices that the wines fetch:

There are both red and white Graves wines. The red is sub-divided into three main categories. The first includes the *crus* of Pontac (Haut-Brion), Lafitte and Château de Margo, which usually produce no more than 300 *tonneaux* and which are considered the best in the whole province. This is normally sold at a price of between 1200 and 1500 pounds a *tonneau*. The majority of the wine is exported to England.

The white wines cover such a range of *crus* that it is impossible to give a comprehensive list of all the different varieties. The wines produced are sold each year at a price of 300 to 500 pounds a *tonneau*, principally to England, Ireland, Scotland, Holland and Germany.

Modern vineyard tractors are well adapted for use in the narrow, low Médoc vineyards.

The third category is of wines whose normal price is from 100 to
200 pounds a *tonneau*, which is widely consumed in Britanny, Nor-
mandy, Picardy, Dunkirk and other northern areas.

The white Graves wines are normally sold at a price of 100 to 200
pounds a *tonneau*, principally to England, Holland, Flanders and
Paris.

More than a century before the great wines of the Médoc and Sauternes were classified, a distinct hierarchy was already in existence. The *Mémoire* of 1730 did not choose to go into the vast number of *crus* which were available; but the distinction made between the main areas for export is obvious, with the better wines naturally going to the richer countries. The scale of prices for the Graves wines which extends from 100 to 1500 pounds a *tonneau* is still relatively accurate if applied to the present-day situation.

It is not by chance that, after centuries of experiment and study, Margaux is now at the top. There was, even at the very beginning, a fortunate combination of the four necessary elements for good wine production. These are, of course, the soil, subsoil, drainage and climate. Their existence attracted people looking for perfection and encouraged them continually to refine production methods. The present-day achievements in planting, growth and vinification are all designed to make the most of this rare composition of natural talents.

> The lands of the Margaux appellation, which include Arsac, Soussans, Margaux, Cantenac and Labarde, not only have the best gravelly soil, which is in the Médoc the first requirement for good wine production, but also have the best hilly contours necessary because of the extraordinary cross-cut made in the larger land mass of gravelly soil by the Jalles du Moulinat range of hills. One might almost say that at the cost of a good quarter of land which has been transformed into swamp, Margaux has in return a group of hills and highlands unequalled in Bordeaux.

This observation by Professor Henri Enjalbert, made with regard to Château Giscours, is in my opinion the best explanation for the excellence of the Margaux vineyards. Glancing at a map of the wine-growing areas within the appellation, one can see the full reality of this layout, which I am tempted to compare to an aircraft carrier whose prow would be Marsac and the stern Cantenac, with Château Margaux as the bridge, and with seven other smaller ships surrounding it as escort. This image seems to convey the idea of these landmasses emerging above the waterlogged marshy ground which guarantees them perfect natural drainage. Without wanting to get immersed in agricultural science, I see the vine being a kind of still turning water into wine. In Margaux, the soil is siliceous (full of pebbles and gravel), and therefore extremely permeable and thin, but rich in oxides and mineral salts. The water table level varies according to the season. At the beginning of the agricultural year the vine has all the necessary water for the development of new vegetation, but this is gradually reduced as the vines mature. For the vines to grow at their best, they must be regularly watered and have plenty of sunshine. The latter can, however, cause dryness in younger vines, but the older plants, whose roots go down as far as 5 or 6 metres, manage to get enough water, but because of their age do not produce a large amount of grapes. The average age of a vineyard is an important factor in the quality of its produce. A vine needs to grow for at least seven years before it begins to produce good grapes and almost fifteen years before they are of the excellent standard required for a quality wine. A vineyard of thirty to fifty years old produces the best wine, and therefore the larger properties are favoured as they are able to renew their vines over a number of years. The best wine-makers are those who, caring little for short-term profit and yield, plan their pruning and re-planting programmes with great patience.

For a long time the average yield per hectare for a Margaux *cru classé* was less than 30 hectolitres. General improvements in agricultural science have gradually increased this average to 40–45 hectolitres. It seems that this may be a level that it would be dangerous to exceed. 'Whenever I see this or that well known appellation ask the INAO to authorize production of 70 hectolitres per hectare, I see this as commercial suicide' (Bernard Ginestet, *La Bouillie bordelaise*, Paris, 1975). On this count, Margaux is one of the most sensible appellations in the Médoc, in Bordeaux, in France, in Navarre and in the world. This discretion can also be dictated by nature, however. Margaux could without doubt justly claim to have the thinnest wine growing soils in all of Bordeaux. The soil there is rich in gravel and pebbles, but extremely low in humus and vegetable matter. It will be possible to improve this with fertilizers, and some owners have done this – and reduced the quality of their product as a result. For the younger plants the best compost in the world is used, which is of course horse manure. When the roots have grown sufficiently deep the vine is left to starve for a short while, and it is this which gives it the necessary qualities to produce the very best wine.

The hills and gravelly terraces in Margaux are composed of alluvial soil. They date back to the relatively recent Pleistocene age. Rarely more than once a century and for only 8000 centuries, an enormous flooding of the Garonne has swept, polished, washed and deposited a huge amount of pebbles and shingle carried from the Pyrenees and the Massif Central. (Another distinctive feature of Margaux, compared to the other Médoc appellations below it – Saint-Julien, Paulliac, Saint-Estèphe – is that its land is made up of a large amount of gravelly soil from the Pyrenees and the Garonne whereas the pebbles in the other areas are, in the main part, from the Dordogne.) This great upheaval effectively sorts the poorer deposits (limestone, granite, etc.) from the good, since the weaker deposits cannot withstand the torrential flooding. What is left is a fine mixture of volcanic and sedimentary minerals, all carefully mixed into a kind of pebble salad. The main constituents are white, yellow or blue quartz, pink and grey quartzite, jurassics, marbled ingots, green-streaked sandstone, black and white flints and lydiens in all shades of grey, green, brown and black.

The Count of Hargicourt was lord of Margaux at the end of the eighteenth century, several years before the storming of the Bastille. He once attended the court of Louis XVI dressed in a coat with buttons which sparkled like diamonds. The other courtiers were so taken with the effect that finally the King's attention was drawn to the sumptuous garment of his colonel: 'My dear sir, you are certainly the most opulent man in my kingdom!' Hargicourt, embarrassed, answered: 'Sire, these are nothing more than the diamonds commonly found on my lands!' The buttons were, in fact, transparent quartz, gathered from among the vines and cut and polished. (One encyclopedia entry reads: 'Paste jewellery is often made of stones from the Médoc, the Rhine and Bristol, where these multi-coloured rock crystals occur naturally, like the pebbles of Cayenne and Alençon, which are all varieties of quartz.')

A similar tale is also told of the Marquis de Ségur at the court of Louis XV. The pebbles in this case would have been from Château Latour. The Marquise Aguado de Las Marismas, who heard the story related about her lands in Margaux, sent the vineyard workers' children in search of these sparkling pebbles for which she paid, according to the nineteenth-century legend, as dearly as if they had been real diamonds. As may be imagined, such folly rendered her notorious throughout the country. As a result, nobody has again exploited this harvest, but 'diamonds' are still found beneath the Cabernets-Sauvignons of Margaux.

Some examples of the pebbles found in the Margaux vineyards, simply polished with abrasive powder. Pebbles such as these are made into necklaces in Antwerp.

Apart from their decorative qualities, their usefulness as a means of aerating the soil and the necessary thinness they give to the land, the gravels and pebbles of the Médoc have a further use: they help to regulate the temperature. Not only do they act as tiny mirrors, reflecting the sun's rays on to the grapes, but they also absorb heat during the day which helps maintain the vines' temperature during the night. It is for this reason that the stakes which support the climbing stems are kept as short as possible, for in this way the harvest can enjoy the full benefit of the natural heat source. This low stature also helps the pickers during the harvest. Such low-growing vines do not occur naturally, as the vine's own inclination is, like a wisteria, to grow higher, as if wishing to outgrow its gardener. (Egyptian paintings depict the grapes being harvested by people reaching high into the air. Roman slaves who were ordered to pick from the highest vines were greatly at risk, and many of them were severely injured in falls.) The Cabernet variety and its more recent offspring, the Cabernet-Sauvignon, are particularly well adapted to growth in gravelly soil. It is the skill of the wine-grower which keeps them to a manageable height. In 1845, Count Odart wrote: 'The practice of skilful pruning to keep the vines to a manageable height is exemplified throughout the Médoc.'

Montesquieu knew the Cabernet as the 'hardy little vine grown in gravelly soil'. Depending on where it is found, it may be known as the Breton, the Véronais or the Arrouya. In Bordeaux, it is also known as Carmenet, Carmenère, Bidure, Vidure or Petite-Vuidure. Several authors describe it as the *Vitis biturica*, better known as the Vigne Bordelaise, which nowadays spreads across the whole of the wine-producing area of western France. I shall leave it to Count Odart to describe it:

It is easy to recognize because of its thin narrow leaves, divided into five pointed, hairless sections: the grapes are medium-sized, rounded and packed close together, very dark in colour and with a peculiar taste; the stalks of the leaves and flowers are dark violet in colour and in winter they become light red, gradually fading to fawn. The wine this variety produces is smooth, rich in bouquet, lightly coloured and long lasting. All the various qualities it possesses fluctuate according to the soil in which it is grown.

In Margaux these qualities are multiplied tenfold, and one might say that this is the perfect combination of vine and soil. The Petit-Cabernet or Cabernet-Sauvignon is to Margaux in the Médoc what the coffee bean is to Blue Mountain in Jamaica. The history of its growth and cultivation goes back to the time of the Gallo-Roman empire and its roots lie in the dim and distant past of Bordeaux. At the very beginning of the seventh century, Archbishop Isidore de Séville, discussing vines and wine, specifically mentions the 'type known as bituric from the name of the area in which it is grown. This plant is extremely hardy and easily survives storms, rain and heat and enjoys great success even in extremely thin soil. In this respect, it is superior to any other.' Ten centuries later, Cardinal Richelieu, well aware of the singular qualities of Petit-Cabernet, transplanted several thousand from the 'Graves de Bordeaux' (of which Margaux was at that time a part) to present them to his intendant, the Abbé Breton. The latter was so successful in spreading not only the word but also the vine, that this variety, renamed 'Breton', became the principal crop in western France, particularly in the Loire valley.

The Cabernet grape can be seen as the basis of every successful Margaux vineyard, but it is certainly not the only important variety. The Merlot grape also has many fine qualities: colour, body, richness in alcohol and smoothness. Less resistant to disease than the Cabernet-Sauvignon, it matures much more quickly, and although it is rarely found in large quantities in Margaux, it is a first-class blending growth. It grows best in well-drained soil and is extremely prone to mildew. Once it has fully ripened, it must be picked without delay. By carefully grading the ripening periods of the Merlot and Cabernet grapes, the vineyard owner is able to bring in his harvest over a convenient period of time. In the best years, the Merlot gives the *cru* an exceptional warmth which combines perfectly with the finesse of the Cabernet. It is probably because of its high sugar content that it is extremely popular with the blackbirds and thrushes. It is from the former, it is said, that the variety takes its name (*merle* being the French for blackbird). The Merlot first appeared in Margaux at the beginning of the nineteenth century.

As well as the Cabernet and Merlot, Margaux produces two other blending varieties: the Malbec (or Malbeck) and the Petit-Verdot. The former was introduced to the Médoc at the end of the eighteenth century, imported from Cahors by M. Malbeck himself. It is particularly well suited to hard, chalky earth, and for this reason is mainly found in the Soussans commune where the chalky subsoil is shallow. The smaller wine-producers are usually fond of the Malbec variety, which gives their wines greater strength and shortens the fermentation

time. Malbec wines soon loose their sediment, and are delicate with a well-defined bouquet. In a larger vineyard their biggest drawback is that the vines are difficult to prune, requiring constant and individual attention.

As for Petit-Verdot, its very name tells us of its distinctive green colour. It is a slow-growing variety whose acidic qualities ensure that any wine into which it is blended will age well. In the eighteenth century there was a great deal of trade with America and thousands of barrels of the better wines were shipped there. The wines which undertook such a long voyage needed to be very robust. At this time the Petit-Verdot came into its own, adding its own distinctive acidic bite to the extreme delicacy of the Cabernet. The Verdot vines are among the first to flower and the last to produce fruit. In Margaux they are only used in small quantities, and during the colder, damper years are not used at all. The Verdot is usually grown on the richer loam soil of the Médoc hills. If the Merlot may be considered as a smoother complement to the Cabernet, the Verdot adds a touch of spice. The wine produced from its grapes alone is almost undrinkable. It is said that no one man can drink a whole bottle alone; there must be at least four people present: one to drink and three to carry him home. It was previously hailed as a powerful diuretic, but it must be said that the Margaux wines quit the body as easily as they enter it, with or without the addition of the Verdot grapes. This is an argument which is seldom touched upon by the shippers.

We must also consider the effects of the extensive grafting of new vines on to old, which practice began after the phylloxera epidemic at the end of the nineteenth century. The scientific study of vines and wine-production has certainly made great steps forward over the last hundred years. The ability to adapt various cuttings to flourish in the microclimate of the area, as well as in varying types of soil and subsoil, is now an important factor in the success or failure of a vineyard. Specialized nurseries supply the grafting plants as required and chosen by the wine-grower. The majority of these come from Blayais or Saint-Emilion where the land is suitable for mass-production. In one method used the cutting is first planted independently and, once it has taken root, is grafted on to the old vine stalk. It was my father, Pierre Ginestet, who introduced this practice in Margaux in the late thirties. He was then owner of Château Rabaud-Promis in Sauternes, where this procedure had become commonplace. It was, however, totally unknown at that time in the Médoc, and he was forced to bring in his steward from Rabaud to Château Margaux, along with a team of wine-growers from Sauterne, who became the pioneers of the new method in Médoc. This method, although it is rather expensive, has many advantages over other types of grafting, but in fact there are few vineyards left which were produced in this way.

In 1983, the final sections of Cabernet-Franc vines, planted direct in 1870, were pulled up. As far as I know, this patch, known as the Orangerie, was the only French vine in the Médoc which managed to resist the phylloxera outbreak. Luckily the vines had already been reproduced through layering and those did not entirely disappear. The oldest vines now existing in the Margaux appellation are probably those of René Renon in Marsac, which date back to his great-grandfather.

The four main stages in the agricultural year leading up to the harvests are pruning, sprouting, blossoming and ripening. Many people maintain that pruning should be done as soon as possible after the leaves of the previous year's growth have fallen. Others recommend waiting until the first frosts have passed. One motto that I have often heard regarding this goes: '*Taille tôt, taille tard – Rien ne vaut taille de mars*' (Prune early, prune late – but there's no point in pruning in March). This advice is certainly useful in the smaller vineyards, and the larger properties prune gradually throughout the winter. From year to year, the motto has proved more or less correct.

The next important stage is when the new leaves begin to shoot, followed by the *mannes*, the tiny bunches of grapes, which are always a good indication of the success of the crop. This is a critical period, during which the spring frosts can, in only a short time, do consider-

After the grapes have been stripped from their stalks and lightly pressed, the pulp and the juice are pumped into the fermentation vats. (This picture is taken at Château Monbrison) ▶

able damage. Most of the larger properties use artificial smoke to prevent damage to the crops by frost. Previously the farmers invoked the '*saints de glace*', St Mamert, St Pancras, and St Servais, as protection against these early frosts. As the Gregorian calendar has now been rejected, the newer saints Estelle, Achille and Jeanne d'Arc are their present-day equivalents. Since this revision it seems that the average temperature in May has risen and the reddish moon which previously foretold disaster has become less threatening. Nowadays, in France, mid-May is usually warmish.

The blossoming period begins at the end of May or the beginning of June and gives the best indication of the success or failure of that year's crop, at least as far as quantity is concerned. There is an old saying that the vines mature approximately one hundred days after blossoming (some say 110 or 115 days after the very first blossom, which is about the same). To calculate it exactly one must work out the date of the height of blossoming, which obviously can be somewhat tricky. In Margaux, this usually seems to be the same day that the first lily appears in the garden. For this reason the kitchen garden at Château Margaux has always contained several lily plants to enable the wine-growers to work out the hundred-day period prior to the harvest. By then all danger of frost will have passed.

It is now that the really critical period begins for the year's crop. The *coulure*, the bad pollination of the flower for whatever reason (degeneration, parasites, bees or, most often, bad weather), always casts its shadow at this time. This effect is also known as *millerandage*. The result is that the tiny grapes remain at the foetal stage and do not grow. At the end of September they remain small, hard and green. This blight can sometimes have a beneficial effect when the harvest becomes too large. In this case, nature has her own way of correcting the problem, as the overloaded vines have difficulty in ripening such a large amount of grapes. In a normal year, however, the *coulure* can drastically reduce the size of the crop. Normally the chestnut trees flower two or three weeks before the vines; if their blossom suffers from *coulure* – which, unlike that of the vines, is visible – it is possible according to local legend to prophesy the failure of that year's crop.

Fifty days after the blossoming, halfway between blooming and maturity, the ripening begins. The grapes begin to change colour and their skin becomes slightly transparent. The older wine-producers call this the 'change'. All this has taken place since April and by now we are well into August. The personality of the new wine is already well established by this stage, as is graphically summed up in a local saying: '*Juin fait le vin – juillet le bouquet – aôut fait le goût*' (June makes the wine – July the bouquet – August brings the taste).

The unique taste of Margaux wine is derived from its discreet complexity. Other areas produce wines with a pronounced character which are thus readily identifiable – like a man with a beard or a big nose. Margaux is the epitome of taste and balance. It is a wine that should be sampled in elegant surroundings for one truly to appreciate the subtle blend of perfumes and tastes. There is absolutely no aggression or violence in its make-up. The bouquet is at the same time both floral and·fruity, a wonderfully harmonious balance. In cold or damp years its delicacy can become rather too marked, but even when not at its best, it remains a true aristocrat. In good years it reigns supreme.

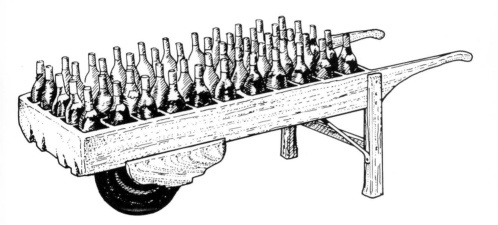

With regard to the lands of the five communes which make up the Margaux appellation area, I have already quoted Charles Cocks, who in 1850 plagiarized William Franck by writing; 'Margaux wines are full of finesse, have a fine colour, a smooth bouquet, they are full-bodied without being heady; they are gentle on the stomach and the head, and leave the breath fresh and the mouth clean.' Franck had already made these points, almost word for word, several years previously. We should not, however, see this as Cocks taking an easy way out, but as, in reality, a confirmation of the reputation enjoyed by Margaux wines in the nineteenth century.

This description has been commonly published in almost all the books on Margaux. Some people quote it verbatim, almost like a well-learned catechism, and no one would presume to apply it to any other area than Margaux. Rather surprisingly, however, I have found the source for this declaration to be the *Topographie de tous les vignobles connus*, published in 1816 by A. Jullien. The author was, in fact, commenting on all Bordeaux wines when he wrote: '... they are really far too well known for anyone to add to their reputation. A first-class

VIN DE MARGAUX

Le Premier Vin du Monde
Véritable élixir de longue Vie

Le Vin de Margaux ranime l'estomac sans fatiguer la tête. L'haleine reste pure et la bouche fraîche, car il a beaucoup de force sans être fumeux. Sa couleur est splendide et il a un bouquet incomparable.

Il est surtout caractérisé par une suprême finesse de goût, qui lui donne une distinction sans égale.

 Acheter du MARGAUX...
c'est acheter
de la JOIE et de la SANTÉ

Bordeaux, well matured, should have a rich colour, plenty of finesse, a smooth bouquet and a taste which fills out the mouth. It should be strong without being smoky and full-bodied without acidity. It should be gentle on the stomach and the head, leaving the breath fresh and the mouth clean.' Could it be then that the Margaux wines have flourished for a century and a half on the reputation of Bordeaux? This is obviously unacceptable and, in fact, the distinction was made by Franck, Cocks and the others who, finding Jullien's praise rather too sweeping to apply to every Bordeaux wine, have restricted its usage to Margaux.

The president of the Syndicat viticole de l'appellation Margaux, Roger Zuger, made a further attempt to pinpoint the qualities of the Margaux produce:

> If Margaux wines can be grouped as a whole because of their similarity in body, they remain, nevertheless, distinctive in the richness and variety of bouquet and tastes which differ widely from

▲ *A prospectus published in the thirties by the Syndicat viticole de Margaux.*

This desolate landscape is a common sight in Arsac, where many gravelly outcrops break up the former green countryside. Much of the gravel has been extracted for building purposes and it is doubtful whether further grape production will ever take place. ▶

château to château. This is obviously a product of the variety of
land available within the area, where certain properties plant on
gravel or sand whereas others have drier or damper conditions . . .
it is all these distinctions taken together which produce the variety
and richness of Margaux.

It is certainly true that there is a great variety of land available, considering the small area covered by the appellation. Each different
gravelly hilltop has a distinctive personality, with a varying outlook
and microclimate. The whole appellation covers about 1100 hectares.
Before it was officially named an appellation in its own right, the
actual area of production within Margaux was much greater. During
the crisis in the 1930s, however, this surface area was reduced, and
since the appellation was granted some good lands have been placed
outside its control. The best example of this is the Château d'Arsac,
which still has the dubious distinction of being classified as an 'Haut-
Médoc' whereas it really deserves to be a *cru bourgeois* in Margaux.
The area of Virefougasse in Soussans is in my opinion unjustly cut off
by the main highway from Margaux to Castelnau. On the edge of
Arsac, there is plenty of typically Médoc land which has been drastically cut back by gravel production. The local authorities have recently
clamped down on this practice, feeling that it is time to preserve these
gravel reserves which, fortified by a reservoir, could produce extreme-

ly good wine. There are obviously other cases where perfectly good land has been cut off from the appellation, but these are now difficult to decide after such a long passage of time. During the 1855 classification the larger properties were favoured because their producing vineyards were wholly incorporated into the appellation, while many smaller landowners were refused permission to use the appellation for their less extensive properties. I think it is high time that the limits of the Margaux appellation were revised and the usage of the name by certain areas not really typical of its produce was cut back.

Of the 57 *crus classés* in the Médoc, shared between Margaux, Saint-Julien, Paulliac, Saint-Estèphe and Haut-Médoc, 22 are in the Margaux appellation, and these 22 are themselves ranged throughout the five classes recorded. These are as follows:

Premier cru	Château Margaux
Seconds crus	Rausan-Ségla
	Rauzan-Gassies
	Durfort-Vivens
	Lascombes
	Brane-Cantenac
Troisièmes crus	Kirwan
	Château d'Issan
	Giscours
	Malescot Saint-Exupéry
	Boyd-Cantenac
	Palmer
	Desmirail
	Dubignon-Talbot*
	Ferrière
	Marquis d'Alesme-Becker
Quatrièmes crus	Pouget-Lassalle
	Pouget
	Le Prieuré-Lichine
	Marquis de Terme
Cinquièmes crus	Dauzac
	Le Tertre

*Dubignon no longer exists

I should add that the names used here are the modern counterparts of the previous designation (for example: Malescot Saint-Exupéry instead of Saint-Exupéry; Marquis d'Alesme-Becker instead of Becker and Prieuré-Lichine instead of Le Prieuré). Pouget-Lassalle and Pouget are also nowadays united under the single name of Château Pouget.

This is a truly outstanding list of medal-winners. One can imagine the whole as a train, drawn by the prestigious locomotive of Château Margaux, followed by a series of carriages where even the fifth class is still extremely luxurious.

Apart from the *grands crus classés*, Margaux also has fifty or so other châteaux, of the more modest *artisan* or *bourgeois supérieur* classifications, which are no less exceptional. I have never been altogether happy with the term '*cru bourgeois*'. Others regard it nostalgically as an aristocratic state to which they were never lucky enough to belong. This division between a *cru classé* and a *cru bourgeois* seems to me rather too severe, as I have attended many blind tastings where the supposedly more modest *petits-bourgeois crus* have been taken for great vintages (and vice versa). Interesting though the 1855 classification is, it would be foolish for any true wine-lover to be overly prejudiced by it. Amongst the 35 *crus bourgeois* of Margaux you are sure to find many delightful surprises which, like their *cru classé* counterparts, leave you with fresh breath and a clean mouth. The wine of Francis Moizeau, for example, a blacksmith in Margaux, is one of the best I have ever tasted.

The smaller wine-producers, those with less than 5 hectares of vineyard, are becoming more and more rare in Margaux. They have had great difficulty surviving through lean years, and the natural exodus to the towns has been especially harmful to the smaller vineyards. Owners of the large properties, having been able to offer steadier employment, have snapped up piece after piece of the smaller lands until today only 10 per cent of the appellation is in the hands of smallholders. Several of the *grands crus classés* have systematically bought back lands which previously belonged to them and had been broken up over the generations. This has obviously been necessary to increase production to meet the greater demand over the years – a situation that is graphically shown by the increase in production in Château Lascombes over the second half of the last century:

1850:	15 *tonneaux*
1868:	16–20 *tonneaux*
1874:	25 *tonneaux*
1886:	35 *tonneaux*

In Féret's *Bordeaux et ses vins* (12th edition, 1969) there appears the
following comment:

> Since this property was bought by the Lichine group in the spring
> of 1952, the Lascombes wines have become some of the most
> popular and respected on the market, notably in the United States,
> where Château Lascombes has become the real ambassador of
> French wines. Through purchasing various new areas and redistri-
> buting production, the property now covers an area of 88 hectares,
> producing some 200 to 270 *tonneaux* a year.

The popularity of Château Lascombes throughout England and
America grew to the point where, in 1971, Bass-Charrington bought

*In Cantenac, Yvan Blanc was the last wine grower to work his property with horses. The horse
retired in 1984, and Yvan Blanc has now joined the team of wine-growers at Château Boyd-
Cantenac, under Pierre Guillemet.*

out Lichine's interest in the property. Nowadays it covers an area of
94 hectares of vineyard and produces some 400,000 to 500,000 bottles
a year. This is an average of almost 400 *tonneaux* a year, representing
40 hectolitres' yield per hectare (still a reasonably low figure). Production has thus multiplied a record 1200 per cent over thirty years
and it is obvious that the increased area of the vineyard has en-
croached on to other Margaux properties.

In 1850 Charles Cocks produced a census with the following
results:

> 19 wine-producers in Arsac
> 13 in Labarde
> 18 in Cantenac
> 43 in Margaux
> 19 in Soussans
> – a total of 112

By 1922, the number of owners within the area of the five communes had gone up to more than 170. (They were not, unfortunately, divided into owners producing on the more typical gravelly soil and those using the richer alluvial loam.)

In 1949, a further survey by Cocks and Féret was produced:

- 38 owners in Arsac, of whom about 30 produced
  1–5 *tonneaux* a year
- 30 owners in Labarde, of whom about 20 produced
  1–3 *tonneaux* a year
- 58 owners in Cantenac, of whom about 20 produced
  1–3 *tonneaux* a year
- 36 owners in Margaux, of whom about 10 produced
  1–5 *tonneaux* a year
- 44 owners in Soussans, of whom about 20 produced
  1–5 *tonneaux* a year

This made a total of 206 wine-producers, excluding the *palus* producers, of which half were classified as smallholders.

Now, over thirty years later, the map has been drastically altered, and the land has been divided up between the *crus classés* and the better *bourgeois crus*. Nowadays the Syndicat viticole de Margaux consists of some 70 owners, about ten of whom have less than 3 hectares.

There has been a considerable restructuring of the properties, and this has necessarily led to the disappearance of a lot of the previous varieties. In my opinion, deterioration in trade in Bordeaux since the last war has been a powerful factor in this change. In the larger appellations the shippers are no longer more important than the actual wine-producers. This has also led to the disappearance of the generic Margaux wines in favour of the better château varieties. The Crédit Agricole has, through an extensive loan scheme, made it possible for the owners themselves to age, bottle and sell their own wines. The richer companies have counter-attacked by buying up some of the better known brands and vineyards, often using foreign capital. Château Lascombes is a good example, though it is by no means the only one. In the same way, what has happened throughout Margaux has been commonplace within the other wine-growing regions. The owners and administrators of the *crus classés* have constantly fought to increase the areas of their lands over the last generation. If people

A sign of the times: once labour-intensive, the whole harvest is now picked by one harvesting machine which can do the work of forty cutters and porters.

asked after the health of Joseph Marsac, who was still producing wine at seventy-eight years of age, it was only to have a better idea of how long it would be before they could have the chance of purchasing his 2½ hectares of Malbec grapes, knowing that his family had no further interest in working the land. Alexis Lichine has, in this case, been a tower of strength, even if he has been disposed to pay off the smaller owners generously in order to gain the very best areas for his property. Lucien Lurton, the Zugers, the Taris and everyone else are determined to enlarge their circle of influence, at the same time increasing the extent of their lands.

Because of this policy, all the *grands crus* have either reconstructed or enlarged their *chais*, cellars and vat-houses, improving the wine-making equipment and increasing their storage capacity. Margaux today boasts a collection of wine-producing buildings and equipment which is perhaps the finest in the world both in quantity and quality. The château-builders of the eighteenth and nineteenth centuries have now given way to the modern wine-temple constructors for whom all must be order, luxury, calm and propriety.

The amount of land owned by the established *crus* has gradually increased over the years and, although they retain the idea of exclusivity, they no longer control this as strictly as they once did. Many of the owners have far larger properties than at the time of the 1855 classification and this has had two effects on the consumer. One is that he has become almost insignificant as an individual, since the wines now have such a large following. The other is that he can make a better choice within a restricted range of products which are all of comparable quality, even if they are dissimilar in all other aspects. All this has helped to promote the idea of increased production in order that everyone can have his or her 75 centilitres of dream wine. Whatever one may think of the publicity tactics employed by the great couturiers and the best chefs of today, they have obviously been extremely effective. I am sometimes left unconvinced by the old-fashioned selling arguments which are still used in the wine-producing world, despite modern methods of production. It really gives one the impression of being in a different century. We all like to be proud of our past, as is only right. We should certainly live in the present and work for the future but we should also educate the consumer to recognize the benefits to him of modern production methods rather than leave him to flounder from lack of information.

There is certainly no doubt, taking everything into consideration, that the wine made nowadays is far better than it was one, two or four centuries ago. There are no more bad years as such; there are only varying vintages. The old custom of lengthy ageing of the wine in

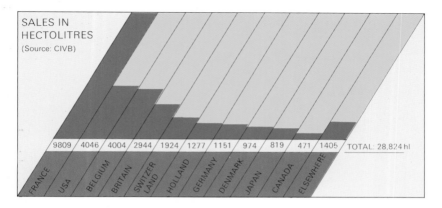

SALES IN
HECTOLITRES
(Source: CIVB)

FRANCE	USA	BELGIUM	BRITAIN	SWITZERLAND	HOLLAND	GERMANY	DENMARK	JAPAN	CANADA	ELSEWHERE	TOTAL: 28,824 hl
9809	4046	4004	2944	1924	1277	1151	974	819	471	1405	

barrels is no longer practised, which is to the benefit of the wine. The new technology employed throughout the wine-producing community, combined with a quality service built on years of experience, is the best guarantee one can offer the consumer. Margaux is at the forefront of this progress and it is time that it was publicized as such.

The market for Margaux wines was extremely restricted even as recently as fifty years ago. Great Britain, Belgium, Holland and the domestic market claimed the lion's share. Nowadays the distribution is much wider and the USA market has by far overtaken the English one. It is largely due to Alexis Lichine that Margaux has achieved such a reputation in America. There is also now, in addition to this, a flourishing market in Switzerland (see the table above).

Every year more and more tourists visit the vineyards at Margaux, right through from April to October and above all at harvest time. Many visit the Maison du Vin du Margaux, which is on the route D2 on the outskirts of the village towards Bordeaux. Here anyone wishing to visit the *chais* can find all the necessary information. One can also buy the latest vintages of several types of wine direct from the Maison. The establishment is used as a *syndicat d'initiative* for all the five communes that form the Margaux appellation. It is run by the Syndicat viticole de l'AOC under Roger Zuger who, like his father before him, is devoted to the area and its wines. Normally, when one wishes to arrange a visit to a vineyard it is best to telephone in advance or to make an appointment through the Maison du Vin. Many of the châteaux do not have a full-time guide and one can easily understand that, if the *maître de chai* is occupied with racking his wines, he is hardly likely to take kindly to receiving a group of tourists. As far as the smallest properties are concerned, it is absolutely essential to make

The Maison du Vin in Margaux is the home of the Syndicat viticole, to which many tourists come before visiting the château. Some of the latest vintages can be bought and sampled here. ▶

an appointment prior to visiting. Visitors are generally extremely welcome, but one should bear in mind that the typical Margaux owner may not always be as jovial or warm as his counterpart in the other wine-growing areas. There are very few opportunities to taste and buy the wine, and if you wish to taste the wine in the *chais*, you will be well advised to take along a loaf of bread and some cheese as a snack, for it is rare to be able to obtain any other form of refreshment. One is always, however, treated with professional candour.

▲ *A head harvester examines the collected produce. He picks out the unripe or rotten grapes and pulls off any leaves still on the bunch. Once the harvest was pre-pressed in the same vats which carried the grapes to the production buildings. This practice has now been discontinued since it caused a rapid oxidization of the crop.*

In Labarde, the Rendez-Vous des Chasseurs restaurant is a good place for either lunch or dinner. ▶

As for the local cooking, this has improved drastically in recent years. Several years ago there was certainly nothing to be found; nowadays, without leaving the Margaux appellation, one can find three good restaurants.

In Labarde: Le Rendez-Vous des Chasseurs. This is easily found since it is near the level-crossing and the small church with its charming bell-tower. The place is simple and clean, and for a very reasonable price one can lunch or dine in style. The menu is usually based around some kind of charcoal-grilled entrecote or a well-cooked casserole. It has a reasonable wine-list, without any outstanding vintages. In short it is an appropriate stop on the way to the vineyards, having lots of local charm and a rustic type of setting which is a fine introduction to the area. There are also ten or so rooms to let.

In Margaux: L'Auberge de Savoie. Beside the Maison du Vin, on the D2 road, M. and Mme Fougeras run a rather more sophisticated establishment. M. Fougeras is in charge of the kitchen while Mme runs the restaurant. There is not a wide choice on the menu but everything is in perfect taste. Treading halfway between traditional French cooking and *nouvelle cuisine*, M. Fougeras lacks neither talent nor invention. He is a true chef, as much at home preparing sauces as roast and grilled meat in their natural juices. His tiny crayfish soufflés 73 make one regret their size. The different meat dishes offered are always appetizing and served piping hot, with a wide selection cooked to perfection (sometimes one may have to wait a little). There is a large variety of delicious desserts all made in the restaurant. The wine list is adequate, based on Margaux wine and various Médoc *crus*. The vintage wines offered are young, but then again this restaurant has not been open very long. The prices are extremely reasonable considering the quality of the food and the service.

In Soussans: Le Restaurant Larigaudière. Leaving the village on the left-hand side, you cannot miss the entrance to Château Haut-Breton Larigaudière which has been newly restored. The chef previously worked at the Chez Philippe restaurant in the Place du Parlement in old Bordeaux. Dominique Pradet was born only three leagues from Larigaudière in Moulis, a small village with its own fine Romanesque church. Initially, the cooking was rather fussy and the bills correspondingly high, but the local clientele have now ensured that there is a much more traditional taste to the dishes prepared here. The prices, too, are now much more reasonable, and one can taste real local cuisine such as snails or lampreys, casseroles or entrecotes, cèpes or salmis. On request, one can even see the master at work. The restaurant is closed annually from 15 November to 12 December. The entrance is extremely impressive; but on no account hesitate to go through it.

In spite of the relative sophistication of Larigaudière, the local cuisine is formed mainly from more simple fare produced in the surrounding area: entrecote steaks and legs of lamb, shad and eels, thrushes and cèpes. Entrecote steak *à la margalaise* is always cooked over a fire of Cabernet vine stalks, usually at least a few months old and two years at the most. The meat is well hung and thickly cut. It is placed on a pre-warmed grill until the embers die down, then it is seasoned with coarsely ground salt and pepper and a few good pinches of chopped shallots. No herbs or mustard or other additives are used to adulterate the natural taste. It is then quickly sliced along the grain and served with baked potatoes or large cèpes. In truth the steak is not eaten, it is rather tasted, like a fine wine, on a warm plate. It is the perfect accompaniment to a good Margaux wine.

The cèpes (wild mushrooms) found in Labarde, Arsac, Cantenac and Soussans are always first-class. In Margaux itself they are extremely scarce, due to the lack of woodland. They are regarded as a delicacy throughout the Médoc, and without any false pride, I am convinced that we produce the very best . . . .

They do, of course, require a certain amount of special attention to keep them at their very best. Mme Germaine Grangerou, the wife of Marcel Grangerou, who was previously *maître de chai* at Château Margaux (following on from his father Marcellus and preceding his son, Jean, who is the present-day *maître*), recommends the following method of preserving them.

The cèpes must be picked during the first quarter of the moon. They should then be placed on clean napkins on the kitchen table. Next the stalks are cut off and cleaned and any dirt is removed before the

In Margaux M. Fougeras, a young master in the art of French cooking, sets the standard for the other restaurateurs in the region.

75

cèpes are delicately peeled. Each head should be individually dried with a clean cloth, above and below. They should then be covered with more napkins and left to dry for a few hours, depending on how damp they are. The cèpes are then placed in a frying pan with the tiniest amount of oil, which has been well heated to drive out any remaining moisture. This should be done for no longer than three minutes either side, and no salt or pepper should be added. The cèpes may then be placed in well-scrubbed jars and left to sterilize for two hours in a large basin of hot water or a boiler. The jars should be left to cool before sorting and the heads and stalks should be separated. To prepare them for eating they should be cooked exactly like freshly picked cèpes: fried in hot oil and seasoned with salt and pepper, garlic and chopped parsley.

The Larigaudière restaurant is situated in the Château Haut-Breton Larigaudière, in the village of Soussans.

This is how Mme Grangerou modestly presents one of the finest traditions of French cuisine. The process may appear simple, but after a few attempts one fully understands its true complexity. It may take two or three years of practice before your cèpes retain their freshly picked taste, but it will be well worth the effort.

The best leg of lamb comes from Arsac, but a good one can always be found in Paulliac or the Bas-Médoc. It should be no bigger than 2½ kilos, and if one has a large number of guests it is better to cook two small legs rather than one large one.

Always ask the butcher to leave intact the tendon attached to the knuckle bone. A good fire should be prepared in the hearth, preferably using old, well-scaled barrel staves. When the fire has taken, and about an hour before eating, the leg is hung over the fire on a thick cord and a wooden splint inserted about halfway down the cord. The top of the cord is attached underneath the mantlepiece or to a trammel if it is to be hung in front of the fire. The bottom of the leg should be about 15–20 centimetres in front of the fire and a dripping pan should be placed about 20–25 centimetres away, with a pebble underneath to tip it slightly forward. The lamb should be spun on the cord about a dozen times and then, like a spring, the cord will keep the leg turning without constant attention. The spinning should be repeated from time to time. While the lamb is still, it should be basted with a mixture of salt and pepper diluted in vinegar and water (at this stage herbs and mustard can also be added to taste). If regularly basted, the skin will be crispy without burning.

The leg should be carved at table and served in large helpings, the juices collected in the dripping pan being served separately in a warmed saucepan. The best accompaniments are steamed green beans, or flageolets or white haricot beans in their juice; or best of all, plenty of freshly picked cèpes. Your dinner party will be a certain success if the whole meal is washed down with a magnum of Margaux wine. If a magnum is not available, use at least three bottles, and should they be of different vintages, always serve the youngest first and the others in order of age.

Shad is commonly to be found in the Garonne, between the time of the vines' first sprouting and their blossoming. It is a superb fish, from the sardine family, but much larger in the Médoc than in Marseille. They are often caught between Macau and Soussans while swimming upriver, using small boats known as '*yoles*', which have both oars and outboard motors. A running net, which should be at least 50 metres long for serious fishing, is used. The most difficult part of the whole process is untangling the net once the catch has been landed.

My own idea of heaven is to spend a fine morning fishing for shad

on the river with a good friend. Afterwards, one can grill the catch over a fire made of vine stalks while the women prepare a fine sorrel purée to accompany the fish. The fish must be carefully sliced along the backbone to remove the tiny bones, although a few are always left because they are so small. All this should be washed down with a good bottle of white Entre-deux-Mers. If one decides to remain faithful to Margaux, a Lascombes rosé will do just as well or, more grandly, a bottle of Pavillon Blanc du Château Margaux, the 'white blackbird' of the red Médoc.

The *'pibales'* (young eels), known as *civelles* throughout the rest of France, are most commonly caught in the small pools near the river from February onwards. They are also exported to Spain where they are served as a delicacy known as *angulas*. They are cooked, still alive, by being placed in boiling oil; they are ready to eat within a minute, requiring only seasoning with salt and pepper. They are eaten warm or cold with vinaigrette.

The thrushes that feed from the vines are one of the most delicious small game birds in the whole of France. It is reported that a fully grown thrush can eat up to three to four times its body weight in grapes each day. It is almost as though one had stuffed them with Margaux! They are normally roasted on a spit over an open fire, or in the oven, stuffed with grapes. To prepare them properly for the oven they should, according to an old recipe, be wrapped individually in greaseproof paper, which is intricately folded to keep in all the juices. (One can probably find the exact method in any book on origami, but if you have a real problem finding something suitable, drop me a line and I'll send you the paper – all you have to do is fold it.) But, to get back to the thrushes, the following recipe is an original by Yves Fougeras, the owner and chef of the Auberge de Savoie in Margaux.

Stuffed thrushes à la margalaise
First bone and clean the thrushes and stuff them with any suitable game stuffing, adding a few truffles if available. Shape them into small round balls and tie up tightly with string. Each bundle should then be thinly wrapped in strips of fat. Heat a small amount of oil in a deep saucepan and add a small piece of fresh lard, allowing it to melt. Place the birds in a pan over a high flame until they are well-browned on all sides. Take a small amount of game stock and lace it liberally with good Margaux wine. Allow this mixture to reduce,

Shad fishing is a traditional pastime in the Haut-Médoc. Salmon are also caught, although in much fewer numbers.

79

The restaurant 'Le Savoie' offers good food in a traditional setting which is at present being extended and renovated. It is a new establishment but one with a fast-growing and well-deserved reputation.

adding mushrooms, a bouquet garni, coarsely chopped parsley and whole cloves of garlic. Finally, remove the strips of fat from the outside of the birds and untie the string. They should then be placed in a circle on a large plate with the mushrooms in the centre. Strain the stock through fine muslin and add lemon juice, a knob of butter and a drop of oil. Coat the birds with this mixture just before serving them nice and hot.

And what would be the perfect accompaniment to such an opulent feast?

Since I was born – under a Cabernet-Franc, one might say – I have heard and read many profanities on which wines should be served with which dishes. There has always been a great thirst for refinement in such matters among amateur gourmets and the gastronomic journalists. Dodin Bouffant, Brillat-Savarin, Prosper Montagné and Curnonsky were well known for their firmly fixed opinions on this topic. These opinions, though acquired, were far from ridiculous. Their literary style rose above their subject matter to a point which makes them a great pleasure to read even today. There is no doubt that the *grande cuisine* is still alive and well and recognized as a true art in itself. If, as far as wine is concerned, you are fundamentally a traditionalist, then this is the course to take in your kitchen. Duck with melon purée, veal *à la menthe* or with sorrel, highly-spiced *mignon de boeuf*, four seasons omelette and a hamburger, all these things can be appealing, at one time or another, to the modern dulled appetite. Whatever one is eating, one ought to choose an appropriate wine for that particular meal. It would be foolish, for example, to attempt to appreciate a good Margaux if one accompanied it with a tandoori chicken. In short, to savour this wine at its best one ought to avoid any foods which are too heavily spiced, sugared, acidic or over-cooked. With these exceptions, Margaux wines go down well with most meals, whatever the meat and however it is cooked. They are also an excellent accompaniment to all cheeses.

In his *Encyclopédie des crus classés*, written in 1981, Michel Dovaz makes the tour of the whole Médoc aristocracy and awards Margaux wines the head of the table. He goes on to draw up an extensive list of dishes, and of the particular variety of Margaux wine best used as an accompaniment. The list is as follows:

Château Margaux	Ris de veau
Château Rausan Ségla	Pigeonneaux belle forestière
Château Rauzan Gassies	Rôti sans sauce
Château Lascombes	Côtes de veau forestières
Château Durfort	Rognons de veau farcis
Château Brane-Cantenac	Pains de ris de veau
Château Kirwan	Carbonnade de veau
Château d'Issan	Carré d'agneau
Château Giscours	Côtes de bœuf à la moelle
Ch. Malescot St-Exupéry	Entrecôte grillée aux sarments
Château Boyd-Cantenac	Cèpes à la bordelaise
Château Cantenac-Brown	Gigot saignant aux haricots très cuits

Château Palmer	Sanglier
Château Ferrière	Nothing
Château Desmirail	Nothing
Château Marquis-d'Alesme	Entrecôte grillée aux sarments
Château Prieuré-Lichine	A bottle of Prieuré-Lichine '67 to oneself (recommended by Alexis Lichine)
Château Pouget	Grives sur canapé
Château Marquis de Terme	Filet de bœuf aux cèpes
Château Dauzac	Epigramme d'agneau
Château Le Tertre	Poularde

This canal forms the border between Margaux and Arcins. It is part of an important reservoir which ensures that the area is kept well drained, a vital element in the production of good wines. It is here that many fishermen come in search of the young eels which are a local delicacy.

In his enthusiasm to cover every eventuality, I think Michel Dovaz has overshot the mark, as it is impossible to fix wine so exactly to any particular dish. The one recommendation which I can whole-heartedly endorse is the bottle of '67 Prieuré-Lichine all to oneself. It seems to me that the French in general are too concerned with the idea of drinking wine only at meal times, not realizing that it is really best enjoyed for itself alone. I know many well-to-do families in northern

In winter, after pruning, the vine stalks are gathered, and any supporting trellis which is damaged is repaired or replaced.

Europe where, having dined earlier, they spend the rest of the evening with or without the television, slowly savouring a fine bottle of vintage wine. Served with small pieces of soft cheese and unsalted biscuits, the full flavour of the wine is more easily distinguishable. Apart from the professional vintners and the drunks under the Pont-Neuf in Paris, I don't know anyone in France who is so dedicated to wine-tasting. In the early sixties, Frank Ténot livened the sound waves of France with his radio show 'For Jazz-lovers'. Having finished the broadcast at around two or three in the morning, he would go home to taste a carefully selected cheese, washed down with a fine bottle of vintage wine. This seems to me a much more fitting manner in which really to appreciate a good wine.

In truth the ideal dish does not exist, nor does the ideal wine. Sometimes one may be lucky enough to find an agreeable combination, or even better, one which borders on a miracle. There are certainly also occasions when one discovers how hideously inappropriate a particular wine may be for a certain dish. In my belief there is no absolute guarantee against such an eventuality. Am I never to sample Château Kirwan if I dislike carbonnade of veal? Every time I have steak, am I forced to drink Malescot St-Exupéry or Marquis d'Alesme-Becker? If the menu contains loin of lamb with *cèpes à la bordelaise*, should I drink a mixture of Château d'Issan and Boyd-Cantenac? The only real way to take such a list is, I feel, with a large pinch of salt!

My own personal advice would be to make the most of the present circumstances and eat and drink whatever seems appropriate at the time. One must always, I feel, please oneself above all in such matters and refuse to be the slave of convention. In restaurants, I have often astonished the *maître d'hotel* by first choosing my wine and then examining the menu for a suitable accompaniment. These things are certainly much easier at home, even with a modest wine cellar. But, whatever you do, never buy a Margaux wine at the last minute and think that it is possible to serve it the same day.

Regarding the various vintages available I have already made two apparently self-contradictory statements. The first is that there is no longer such a thing as a 'bad' vintage. The second is that Margaux wines are extremely sensitive to climatic variations. These two facts do, however, bear each other out. This has been made possible by modern methods of production which have, to a large extent, helped to overcome the deficiencies and inconsistencies of the weather. It is also true to say that, from one year to the next, there is a much greater fluctuation in the characteristic qualities of wines produced in Margaux than in the majority of the other appellation areas. Margaux remains capable of capturing all or some of its distinctive qualities in any one year and, whatever the outcome, it is always exceptional.

I am in no way obsessed with the need for a lengthy ageing process. The real honours for young wine must go to Beaujolais, but I am well aware that there are pleasures to be derived from drinking a young Margaux. There are many wine-lovers in Bordeaux who would not dream of touching a drop of Médoc wine less than ten years old. The English are even more conservative, as can be seen from the success of sales of very old vintages at Christie's in London. It is important, however, not to confuse such collectors' pieces with the works of art that our humble wine-makers provide for us every year. The year after bottling is certainly a critical period: it is advisable, in most cases, to wait at least twelve months before opening a new wine. This used to be much longer. The wines went through their 'bottle-sickness' period for a longer time, suffering from secondary fermentation. It was impossible to predict when this sickness would strike, making the wine slightly gassy and murky in colour, with an unpleasant bouquet and change in flavour. This period usually lasted several months, sometimes up to one or two years. Nowadays the sickness follows on directly from the fermentation period, and once bottled the wine is usually no longer at risk from such adverse reactions. Nevertheless, there is still a lot to be said for leaving the wine to rest after bottling.

The lesser vintages should be drunk rather sooner, since they are prone to a loss of body over a long period. They can, however, be extremely delicious, and my grandfather often remarked: 'I would much rather drink a *grand cru* of a lesser vintage than a *petit cru* of a great one.' Without taking this too literally, there is certainly pleasure to be had in drinking a good Margaux wine from a lesser year, when it has been aged for three or four years. It strikes me as being a kind of rich Beaujolais.

Most wine-lovers are enthusiastic about vintage lists which compare the produce from one year to the next, giving each a star rating. These can certainly be useful guides, but it would be foolish to take them as gospel. However, in the interests of simplicity, I have devised a small scale below which is extremely helpful in working out the correct ageing period for a particular vintage.

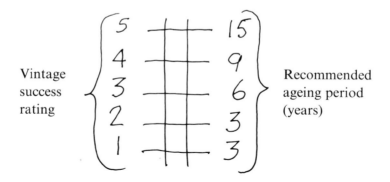

At the bottom of the scale, the number of years indicated is an optimum rather than a minimum. At the top of the scale, the reverse is true. *In medio stat virtus.* A Margaux wine produced in an average year is drinkable after about six years. A good year, like 1975, will be at its best in thirty years.

▲ *The willow twigs which were traditionally used to tie the vines are now gradually being replaced by synthetic materials. Young willows were previously planted in the richer loam soil areas and beside the streams to provide these twigs, or* vimes *as they are called.*

◄ *Pruning the older vines is a real art. Here, at Château du Tertre in Arsac, the vines are pruned and tied to follow exactly the growth pattern desired.*

89

Thirty years ago the '53 and '55 vintages were produced, which are the stars of today. Thirty years ago, the vineyards were worked with horses and oxen. Thirty years ago, the wines were aged for more than two years in the barrel and then bottled entirely by hand: corked, sealed, labelled, wrapped (in paper) and cased (in straw). When the wines of the '75 vintage are at their best, the century will also have changed. Who can predict what methods of cultivation and vinification will be current at that time? Machines have already invaded the vineyard and the *chai*. Some of the Margaux owners are now using machines to harvest the grapes. We must move with the times, and the speed essential if the grapes are to be picked at their very best is something only a machine can truly accomplish. There are still certain disadvantages since the machine often strips the vine leaves, but improvement is simply a matter of time and development. We already have machines for fertilizing and spraying, and one day soon pruning will also be mechanized. Microprocessors have made great progress in the world of wine as they have throughout other industries. One might even one day see a machine used for tasting which, sufficiently programmed, would be able to describe its findings as fluently as any oenologist. For the moment, however, this is one phase which is best left to the experts.

Many of the methods used in wine production have changed over the years, but the distinctive sight of the workers pruning the vines remains unchanged over the centuries.

The taster thus progresses, from one wine to the next, from one book to the next, from step to step. His knowledge gradually broadens and deepens. Over many years scientific developments have been made which, thanks to the efforts of Le Magnen and Vedel, have given us a precise vocabulary for the description of our gustatory sensations. The art of writing on wine has also been perfected stylistically by such writers as Chauvet, Coste, Goffard and Puisais. (Emile Peynaud: *Le Goût du vin*, 1980)

It may not always seem that progress is for the best, but in spite of this I am drawn to paraphrase Professor Peynaud in declaring that 'the art of Margaux wine-making has been perfected by Boyer, Guillemet, Lurton and Zuger'. Margaux cannot escape the winds of change. On the contrary, its best path is to set an example to the rest of the wine-growing world. Certainly, up to now, there is no indication that it is ready to resign its crown.

Ausonius once wrote to his friend Théon:

I must humbly apologize for not having written to you earlier, my friend Théon. We have just gone through a rather hard winter and I am at present pondering the benefits of spring, without any suitable companion to share my thoughts. I realize that the Bordeaux Academy did me a great honour in asking me to be head of the rhetoric department, ably assisted by Acilius Glabrio, Nepotiamus, Victorius and a large number of sub-intellectuals whose ignorance is as immense as their pretensions to intellectuality.

I am, at the moment, well and truly tired of them and look forward to your company to give me a new lease on life. It is not too late in the season for you to gather three hundred or so of those exquisite little oysters found in the sea, between Domniton and Noviomagus. You know well that I am capable of eating at least half of such an amount myself. I will take care of all the other provisions necessary. Philon will bring up my wine from Lucaniac and I will tell Valentinus to save me four ducks, and one can always rely on our friend Julius to provide the rest.

Please come as quickly as possible by boat; you will find it easy to get to Bordeaux this way, as far as Thermes Marojaliques. Here in this peaceful spot, far from the hustle and bustle of the big city, I await your arrival within the next twelve days. Your friend. Ausonius.

I cannot personally guarantee the authenticity of this document, but the details within it would seem to be in accord with what we already know of this great poet. There are, however, many gaps in our knowledge of him.

The 'Thermes Marojaliques', previously known as 'Marojallia', are the seventh of Ausonius' eight properties listed by Jullian, Piper, Schenkl and Etienne. The actual site has never been exactly located until now, but there is much evidence to support the theory that Margaux was, in the ninth century, a Gallo-Roman spa town. Its location corresponds to descriptions given by Ausonius of his travels, which were predominantly made by water. Bec d'Ambès, where the Garonne and the Dordogne meet, was further upstream at the time, and Margaux was almost directly opposite Bourg. The ports of Macau and Margaux were very busy, and had almost daily dealings with the town of Bourg (Burgus). I think that there is also truth in the theory which locates Ausonius' main house on the banks of Bourg. In this way Ausonius could easily intend to spend some time at Marojallia before crossing the estuary back to Bourg to oversee his most important lands.

If toponymy can be considered an exact science, the phonetic change of Marojallia to Margaux is quite likely. There is a place in Margaux called Maragnac. The main river of the commune, Lestonat, was once known as Magnole. The central part of the modern town, between the town hall and Château Malescot, was once known as La Maillolle. All of these seem to bear witness to the original name of 'Marojallia', Ausonius' holiday home. Château de La Mothe, which was the name of the building prior to Château Margaux, was built between the thirteenth and fourteenth centuries, right next to the river. This would place it on the left bank of the Garonne, approximately a kilometre further south-west than today. 'Marojallia' (or Maillolle) must have been large enough to accommodate the buildings necessary for coastal trading. It is known that from the seventeenth century onwards there was so much build-up of silt in this harbour that the

Throughout the pruning period the old vine stalks are disposed of by burning. But all the wine-growers retain a few faggots over which to cook their steaks.

public authorities were obliged to open up other ports to serve Margaux. Besides this, there is a large amount of limestone rock in the Margaux area, which is unique in this part of the Médoc. This is formed into a thick bed of lakeside chalk, known as 'Plassac'. This geological phenomenon produced the spring at La Fontanelle, which has run freely since Ausonius' time and which provided the purest water in the area. Near the source of the spring one can see many traces of a much older construction which has long been disused.

In short, I am convinced that the 'Thermes Marojaliques' where Ausonius entertained his friends was not far from plot 165, section A, of the cadastral survey of Margaux ... it only remains for a detailed excavation to be undertaken to solve the matter.

History may have been manipulated a thousand and one times, but the people of Margaux remain true magicians. Through the centuries they have, with an artistry rivalling that of Robert Houdin with his magic hat, produced and made vanish many different *crus*. The marquis was replaced to profit the viscount. This latter designed an impressive vineyard and constructed a home worthy of an archduke. Only a few years later the lands were swept clean, and many of the Médoc *grands crus* have known such losses and gains of fortune and popularity over the years. If one was asked to draw up a plan to restore the original properties as classified in 1855, the whole area would be devastated.

These changes and acquisitions should be seen as a slow but steady change for the better over many generations. Within the area nowadays known as the AOC Margaux a great deal of property has changed labels, having been regrouped with the *crus classés* or the main *crus bourgeois*. The idea of extending these great properties is, for the most part, a good one, since it has effectively raised the average quality of the product. We have seen history made by the likes of Aulède, Rausan, Lascombes, Brane and Kirwan, and now we see it continued by the present-day owners.

Making great wine is still a personal vocation and the members of the Margaux school are the most dedicated students of this art.

The *Crus*

The term '*cru classé*' is used only in describing the *crus* which were part of the official 1855 classification. This date is not repeated each time the classification is mentioned.

The number of coloured glasses beside the name gives an idea of the quality of the wine in relation to its selling price. This measurement, which has been made objectively, is naturally subject to fluctuation. It should be taken as a rough guide to the quality rather than constituting a formal classification.

Certain varieties use one or more secondary labels to denote the second product of their property. These 'second varieties', which are mentioned in this list, are followed by an arrow which indicates the main variety.

This symbol shows that a particular variety is a second product of a larger property.

Angludet (Château d')

cru exceptionnel

Main areas: Cantenac and Arsac **Owner:** Société civile Château d'Angludet **Director:** Peter A. Sichel, aided by Michel Chauvet **Surface area of vineyard:** 32 hectares (total property 80 hectares) **Average age of vines:** 16 years **Grape production:** 50% Cabernet-Sauvignon, 35% Merlot, 8% Cabernet-Franc, 7% Petit-Verdot **Production:** 100,000 bottles **Local sales:** Tel (56) 88 71 41, **and by mail order** (France only): M. et Mme Peter A. Sichel, 33460 Margaux **Retail sales:** Maison Sichel, 19 quai de Bacalan, 33300 Bordeaux

Of all the noble houses of Margaux, Angludet is one of the oldest. Nowadays administratively linked to Cantanac, Angludet previously included part of Arsac and at that time its total surface area was much greater than the present 80 hectares.

In the purest medieval tradition, the gentlemen of Angludet were proud and quick to take offence, and from as far back as the twelfth century, Bertrand d'Angludet was celebrated as Médoc aristocracy. Two centuries before the Battle of Marignan, in 1313, a member of the Angludet family blithely refused to swear his loyalty to the powerful Baron de Blanquefort. He was welcomed with open arms by Edward II of England, both for his courage and for the excellent produce of his vineyard.

Until the French Revolution, the château was ranked as a *'cru classé'*, its wines being as expensive as the present third and fourth *crus* of Médoc. At this time the vineyard was the property of a certain M. Legras who, in a fit of political ardour, renamed his produce 'La République'. His four children were thus protected by the law of the new republic and in 1791, following the death of their father, they divided the property into four parts, along with the good reputation of the wine. And so the Legras demonstrated their extreme patriotism, although Angludet remained unclassified in 1855.

For almost a century after this the fortunes of the family fluctuated wildly. In 1892 Jules Jadouin brought a much-needed unity to the running of the property, and with the succession of his son-in-law, Jacques Lebègue, in the early twenties Angludet came back into its own. This state of affairs did not last long, however; the vineyard went through bad times in the thirties and forties, when its owner, M. Six, an industrialist from the north of France, was more interested in the butter and eggs sent to him by his farmer each week than in the well-being of the vineyard. These troubles were followed by further difficulties in the fifties when Mme Rolland, who also owned the Château Coutet at Barsac, had her newly replanted vineyard destroyed by frost. In 1960, Lucien Lurton bought up half the vines and the other half became English property once more, being bought by Maison Sichel.

Peter and Diana Sichel are the present-day owners of Angludet, and thanks to them it is once more on the road to success. Swans and ducks may now be seen swimming on the enlarged stream, and the softly sloping lawn would do justice to Wimbledon. On summer weekends the family play cricket there, especially when Ted Harris, a brother-in-law, arrives with his 'big kids'. A swimming pool, a cottage, a tennis court and some Welsh ponies complete the country scene. If you are taken to visit the *chai*, the wine storehouse, you will be understood if you speak English.

The vineyard, surrounded by Giscours, Brane-Cantenac and Kirwan, is on a fine plateau of gravelly banks where even the couch-grass is unable to grow. The vines reign supreme. Six *crus* of Médoc, unfairly overlooked in the classification of 1855, obtained permission from the Bordeaux courts in 1932 to classify themselves officially as a *'cru* 97

At Angludet the vines extend across a romantic landscape, reminiscent of Britain.

exceptionnel'. Angludet was one of these. The wine produced by Angludet is surprisingly lively for the Margaux appellation. It is rich in colour, dry and good value. Truly a wine of connoisseurs.

Baudry (Château) 🕯 → *Desmirail*   🍷 🍷 🍷 🍷 🍷

Bel Air-Marquis d'Aligre (Château)

cru exceptionnel

Main areas: Soussans and Margaux **Owner:** Pierre Boyer, 33460 Margaux. Tel (56) 88 70 70 **Surface area of vineyard:** 17 hectares (total property 40 hectares) **Average age of vines:** 35 years **Grape production:** Red **Production:** 'negligible' says the modest M. Boyer **Retail sales**

These stamped bottles were the height of fashion in the nineteenth century.

This is another variety which was overlooked in the 1855 classification. Perhaps one might say that the members of the jury of the World's Fair organized by Napoleon III were fearful of giving too much praise to the Margaux wines. Bel Air-Marquis d'Aligre is a *cru exceptionnel* and its right of appellation Margaux was legally recognized in March 1898. The production buildings are based at Soussans and the vineyard is tucked away between Margaux and Soussans.

Pierre Boyer is a purist. He has no qualms about sacrificing quantity to quality, and, as a result, the wine is of the very best quality. Vines are maintained at an average age of 35, which in itself is an indication of the worth of this vineyard. In this respect, Pierre Boyer follows in the footsteps of his predecessors who likewise sacrificed material gain for the quality of the wine. During the whole of the nineteenth century not a drop of Bel Air-Marquis d'Aligre was sold commercially. The Marquise of Pomereu and the Marquis d'Aligre produced wine solely for their own tables and as gifts for their many friends. Only a handful of Parisian restaurateurs were allowed to subscribe.

The bottles were remarkable in having a moulded stamp on the neck (only the very best *crus* had such marks at the time). In the same way an inscription was moulded on the back of each bottle: 'Not to be taken away'. As a result it became customary for those in the know to refer to Château Bel Air-Marquis d'Aligre as 'forbidden Margaux'.

These days Pierre Boyer is happy to allow the wine to be tasted, but there will never be enough for everyone. It is a lively wine, rich and usually very fruity, with at times a hint of liquorice – a sure sign of quality in a good wine cellar.

Bellegarde (Château) ♟ → *Siran* ♟ ♟ ♟ ♟ ♟

Bigos (Clos de)

Main area: Soussans **Owner:** André Mestrie, who oversees both direction and production **Surface area of vineyard:** 0.8 hectares **Average age of vines:** 30 years **Grape production:** 1/3 Merlot, 1/3 Cabernet-Sauvignon, 1/3 Cabernet-Franc

---

Bory (Château) ⚑

→ Angludet

Bouquet de Monbrison

cru artisan

Main area: Arsac **Owner:** Roland Barreau, who oversees both direction and production. Tel (56) 88 72 87 **Surface area of vineyard:** 3 hectares **Average age of vines:** 25–30 years **Grape production:** 45% Cabernet-Sauvignon, 20% Cabernet-Franc, 25% Merlot and Malbec, 10% Verdot **Production:** 15,000–18,000 bottles **Local sales and by mail order:** It is always worth trying **Retail sales**

Boyd-Cantenac (Château)

3ᵉ cru classé

Main area: Cantenac **Owner:** GFA des Châteaux Boyd-Cantenac et Pouget **Managing agent and director:** Pierre Guillemet, who looks after the cultivation and wine-making under the direction of Professor Emile Peynaud **Surface area of vineyard:** 18 hectares (total property 26 hectares) **Average age of vines:** 30 years **Grape production:** 67% Cabernet-Sauvignon, 7% Cabernet-Franc, 6% Petit-Verdot, 20% Merlot **Production:** 85,000 bottles **Local sales:** Tel (56) 88 30 58, **and by mail order** (France only): Château Boyd-Cantenac, Cantenac, 33460 Margaux **Retail sales:** Dubos Frères, André Quancard, Moueix-Export, Descaves, Bruck-Cruse-Diffusion, Gautreau, Barrière, Coste, Eschanauer – all in Bordeaux.

It is sometimes difficult for the layman to make a choice from an extensive wine list. Even the restaurateur himself can be confused by the different labels, but here at Cantenac three *crus classés* are well known even to foreign ears. They are, of course, Boyd-Cantenac, Brane-Cantenac and Cantenac-Brown.

The Brane vineyards extend, almost like a private garden, to the front of the château.

In 1754, Jacques Boyd, the King's equerry, who lived in the suburb of Chartrons in Bordeaux, bought some land in the parish of Cantenac. It was on these lands that the Boyd family established their vineyard and allied themselves with the Browns. It was a complicated business. The judges in the 1855 classification looked into the wider-ranging aspects of the case in placing Boyd's wine in the category of a *3ᵉ cru*. Five years later, this judgement was clarified in favour of Brown-Cantenac and, as a result, Boyd's fortunes went into a deep decline. It was Fernand Ginestet who, after Abel Laurent, restored the variety to its previous reputation, and Pierre Genistet, his son, was the discreet architect of this new success. Just as in Pauillac the vineyards of the Baron de Pichon Longueville (*2ᵉ cru classé*) had been divided into two distinct *crus*, Baron and Comtesse de Lalande, the property bought by Jacques Boyd was recognized as having produced three.

Boyd-Cantenac today belongs to the Guillemet family. Pierre Guillemet is a dedicated wine-grower who knows every inch of his land and vines. The *cru* is predominantly produced from Cabernet-Sauvignon grapes which are of an age to produce a small amount of high-quality wine, full of finesse and charm. I must add that Professor Emile Peynaud adds his own drop of scientific expertise in the vats during the wine-making process.

One might be tempted to reproach Boyd-Cantenac for the simplicity of its label. Such modesty, however, being rare these days, should invite our admiration; after all, one does not judge a book by the cover.

Brane-Cantenac (Château)

2e *cru classé*

Main area: Cantenac **Owner:** Lucien Lurton **Chef de culture:** Yves Camelot **Maître de chai:** Yves Blanchard **Surface area of vineyard:** 85 hectares (total property 300 hectares) **Average age of vines:** 25 years **Grape production:** 70% Cabernet-Sauvignon, 15% Cabernet-Franc, 13% Merlot, 2% Petit-Verdot **Production:** 300,000 bottles **Local sales:** Tel (56) 88 70 20, **and by mail order** (France only): Château Brane-Cantenac, Cantenac, 33460 Margaux **Retail sales:** All the main shippers of Bordeaux

In 1693, Bertrand de Brane was the King's adviser and Lord Chancellor at the court of Aydes in Guyenne. His son, Joseph, had the distinction of owning a *cru* in the Pauillac commune. This *cru* was called Brane-Mouton but a century later it assumed its present name of Mouton-Rothschild. At that time the château of Brane-Cantenac was known simply as Gorce (or Gorse). It was Hector, Bertrand's grandson, who earned the nickname 'Napoléon des vignes'. He reigned supreme over his empire, and was, in fact, the first to organize wine production in the modern sense. He appears to be the one we have to thank for the modern Cabernet-Sauvignon. Having sold Mouton, Hector bought the Gorce *cru* and invested large sums of money in its production. In 1838 he wrote: 'I believe that what I have created should bear my own name. The name of Gorce is widely known, both in Bordeaux and abroad, but that of Brane is no less celebrated... I intend gradually to rename the Gorce *cru* and take it under the patronage of Brane-Cantenac.' This he did with great success and, over the next thirty years, he became famous within the world of wine-production for his dedicated professionalism. This success, however, was not enough to guarantee the property economic stability and Hector's son, Jacques Maxime, sold the Château in 1866.

The stony hilltops of Château Brane-Cantenac are among the highest of the Margaux appellation. They have an almost uniform depth of 10–12 metres. At the beginning of the century the property belonged to the Société des Grands Crus de France, who also owned about ten other vineyards including Coutet, Issan and Lagrange. The Récapet-Lurton family, who had been shareholders in Château Margaux since 1922, bought up the whole Brane-Cantenac property in 1926 when the Société des Grands Crus auctioned its possessions. Today Lucien Lurton, François's son, owns this great *2ᵉ cru classé*, the only one in the Cantenac commune to be classified and one of the five with the Margaux appellation. Lucien Lurton is a present-day 'Marquis de Carabas' of the vineyard, reigning over 430 hectares (the whole commune of Margaux is only 630 hectares) which contains some 145 vineyards with such marks as Château Brane-Cantenac, Château Durfort-Vivens, Château Desmirail, Château La Tour de Bessan, Château Notton-Baury, Domaine de Cure-Bourse, Domaine de Fontarney.

If you wish to make a complete tour of the property, you should visit such places as Château Villegeorge at Avensan, Château Bouscaut at Cadaujac, Château Haut-Nouchet at Martillac, Château Climens at Barsac, Château Doisy-Dubroca at Barsac, Château de Camarsac at Camarsac and other places uncovered at low tide, where you would have to wear Bermuda shorts to harvest the Malbec grapes.

Lucien Lurton is without doubt a pioneer in modern wine production. He rules far and wide and lives intensely. He is certainly more of an untiring conqueror than a lover of peace and calm. I wonder if, contemplating all the jewels of his crown, he remains nostalgic for Château Margaux? This *cru* is, perhaps, the only one he may judge worthy of himself but, all the same, three *cru classés* at Margaux are not something one finds everywhere. There is plenty there to fill one's life – and more than 2000 casks!

Brane-Cantenac is a delicate, silky, tender wine, and although by nature a little capricious is always ultimately congenial.

Cantenac Brown (Château)

3ᵉ cru classé

Main area: Cantenac **Owner:** Société civile du Château Cantenac Brown **Director:** Aymar du Vivier, who also takes care of the cultivation **Maître de chai:** Willy Przybylski **Surface area of vineyard:** 31 hectares (total property 33 hectares) **Average age of vines:** 25 years **Grape production:** 75% Cabernet-Sauvignon, 8% Cabernet-Franc, 17% Merlot **Production:** 90,000 bottles **Local sales:** Tel (56) 88 74 37 **Retail sales:** Maison de Luze, Quai des Chartrons, Bordeaux (up to the 1984 vintage)

> *Ce Château grâcieux que baigne l'eau d'un lac,*
> *Est un troisième aussi, c'est le Brown-Cantenac.*
> *Ce sol dont vous voyez, de loin, poindre la crête,*
> *Fut bien longtemps, hélas! battu par la tempéte!*
> *Jouet infortuné d'avides créanciers,*
> *Il a souvent gémi sous le pas des huissiers,*
> *Mais rien ne put flétrir une terre si noble;*
> *Plus riche que jamais reverdit le vignoble.*

These lines, written by the untiring versifier of Médoc, Biarnez, just before the Franco-Prussian war of 1870, aptly reflect the joys and sorrows of several of the Bordeaux châteaux which, over the years, have known shame and glory through economic upheaval and mismanagement.

The château itself was previously cut off from the vineyards and divided into apartments, but the Du Vivier family have recently bought it back, thus rejoining the head to the body of this fine property. It was designed by the celebrated animal painter John Lewis Brown, son of a family of British wine merchants and friend of Henri de Toulouse-Lautrec, with whom he shared an equal passion for good wine, young women and his *grand-maître* Princeteau. But, talented though he was, John Lewis Brown was unable to make a living from his painting; he was forced to sacrifice his wine

Château Cantenac Brown is one of the architectural curiosities of the region.

for his daily bread and in 1843 sold off his property in two lots. The Lalande family from Chartres were at that time well known and at the height of their prosperity. They bought out Brown for a pittance and moved in with their army of domestic staff, leading a wild social life. From the vine to the vat, from the vat to the barrel and from bad to worse, the inheritor of this saga, Jean Lawton (the best snipe-shooter in north Bordeaux) decided to sell the vineyard to the Du Vivier family, its present owners. Aymar du Vivier and his guardian angel, Marie-Ange, have taken Brown in hand and given it the treatment it truly deserves. There are three basic conditions which contribute to the success of a business: the will, the ability and the knowledge. Aymar and Marie-Ange du Vivier have all three. Cantenac Brown, today a challenger, must soon resume its rightful position as leader. Take my tip and back this 3^e cru.

Canuet (Château)

cru bourgeois

Main area: Margaux **Owners:** J. and S. Rooryck **Director:** J. Rooryck **Steward:** S. Rooryck **Chef de culture:** Raymond Martin **Maître de chai:** Ch. Rodriguez **Surface area of vineyard:** 10 hectares (total property 10 hectares) **Average age of vines:** 16 years **Grape production:** Red **Production:** 50,000 bottles **Local sales:** Tel (56) 88 70 21, **and by mail order** (France only): Château Canuet, 33460 Margaux **Retail sales:** The Roorycks have their own retail outlet

When a Fleming meets a native of Champagne, the result is a Canuet. The Rooryck family have been in Margaux since 1919. Jean Rooryck began by breathing new life into the Château Labégorce cru. After his mother died the property was sold, and Jean and Sabine Rooryck bought a pretty house in the middle of the village which was once known as Canuet. The result of patient restoration work is 10 hectares of good vines endowed by the surrounding crus classés. Although some of the vines are still a trifle young, they are well looked after and, according to the character of the vintage, one can find wines which are either strong and full bodied or fine and delicate. The vinification process is long enough for the tannins to do their work without producing an excess of acidity. Resurrected as cru bourgeois, the Château Canuet regularly wins gold and silver medals at agricultural fairs. Its relatively modest price makes it a good choice.

Carabins (Château des)

→ *Ligondras*

Sabine Rooryck, smiling and dynamic, oversees production at Canuet.

Castelbruck (Cru de)

cru artisan

Main area: Arsac **Owner:** Marc Raymond, who oversees both direction and production **Surface area of vineyard:** 3 hectares (total property 3.5 hectares) **Average age of vines:** 8–10 years **Grape production:** Traditional **Production:** Approximately 50 hectolitres per hectare **Local sales:** Tel (56) 30 42 73 (about a quarter of each harvest is bottled on site) **By mail order** (France only): Cru de Castelbruck, Le Tayet, Macau, 33460 Margaux **Retail sales:** Three-quarters of the production is sold to various shippers

Marc Raymond is the third generation of a wine-growing family. The family property is at Macau, where their Château des Charmilles produces an agreeable 'Bordeaux *supérieur*' in the rich loam soil. Things could have continued in this way and Marc Raymond would then have had no place in these listings. But, in his eyes, it was a crying shame to live so close to the appellation Margaux and to have no other benefit from it than sharing the occasional bottle with friends. He thought it a pity to be involved in wine-growing without having access to the best lands. Finally he regretted that he was unable to demonstrate his skill in planting, pruning, fertilizing and harvesting Cabernet-Sauvignon outside his own territory. Over the last ten years Marc Raymond has built up a small appellation Margaux vineyard, broken up into eight parts throughout the Arsac Commune, where two of them border on *grands crus classés*. This relatively young wine is now coming into its own.

Charmant (Château)

cru *1er artisan*

Main area: Margaux and Soussans **Owner:** René Renon, who oversees both direction and production **Surface area of vineyard:** 5 hectares (total property 6 hectares) **Average age of vines:** 50% of the vineyard is 100 years old **Grape production:** 45% Merlot, 50% Cabernet, 5% Petit-Verdot **Production:** 20,000 bottles **Local sales:** Tel (56) 88 35 27, and by mail order (France only): Château Charmant, 33460 Margaux **Retail sales:** Maison Joanne, Carignan, 33370 Tresses

This little vineyard has been situated between Margaux and Soussans since the beginning of the nineteenth century. In 1886, Charles Cocks referred to the '*cru* Charmant' belonging to B. Constantin and placed it in merit among the best *crus artisans* and *crus paysans*. At that time it was also known as Constant-Charmant. Its present owner, René Renon, is the kind of man now rarely found in Margaux. He is, by definition an '*artisan supérieur*'. He lives with his vines, for his vines and by his vines. He is fluent in the local patois, and can recount numerous local anecdotes when he feels so inclined. He certainly has no need of a weather forecast to know what the weather will be like. He and his wife Jeannette manage their two *crus artisans*, Château Charmant and Château La Galiane, surrounded by the *grands crus*. One might perhaps think that the term 'château' is less apt than the former designation of '*cru*'. One might also find that the label has a look of Château Margaux about it, but one would be wrong to assume that this was a deliberate act on the part of the owner, who is more than modest regarding his prestigious neighbours.

Half of the vineyard is more than a hundred years old, and although it is difficult to be exact, I think these are the oldest vines in Margaux. The most remarkable thing about them is that they are the original plants (that is to say, not grafted) of Cabernet and Merlot with a few Carmenères. It was René's father, Adonis Renon, who taught him how to prune the vines. They give very little wine because of their age, but it is of the finest quality – full-bodied and subtle and sometimes, when properly aged, close to matching the most celebrated *crus* in the country.

Clairefont (Ch.) ⚱ → Prieuré-Lichine

Clos de La Gravière (Château)

cru *artisan*

Main area: Arsac **Owner:** M. and Mme Mondon, Les Châlets, 33480 Avensan, Tel (56) 58 20 67 **Surface area of vineyard:** 2.7 hectares (total property 30 hectares) **Average age of vines:** 25 years **Grape production:** 1/3 Cabernet, 1/3 Cabernet-Sauvignon, 1/3 Merlot **Production:** 1000 bottles produced on site, the remainder sold to various shippers **Local sales:** Practically none, **and by mail order** (see below) **Retail sales**

Avensan is a commune bordering on both Soussans and Arsac. It is composed equally of forest and vines. There are several good *crus bourgeois* and *crus artisans* to be found there under the appellation Haut-Médoc.

M. and Mme Mondon live on the family property which they cultivate themselves. Mme Mondon is originally from Arsac and she inherited the land, of which about 3 hectares are divided between production of Cabernet, Cabernet-Sauvignon and Merlot grapes. The average age of the vine stock is 25 years and Mme Moudon's uncle, the Provost of Arsac, should be happy to see from on high that his vines are well tended and his wine is well made. Nothing is perfect, however, and I find it particularly regrettable that the quantity of each harvest reserved for bottling on site is so small. A thousand bottles is hardly sufficient. One must take positive action, and I suggest that you write to Mme Mondon, after the harvest, asking her to reserve two or three cases. She could hardly refuse you.

Cure-Bourse
(Domaine de) 🍷

→ Durfort-Vivens

Dauzac (Château)

5ᵉ cru classé

Main area: Labarde **Owner:** SAF Chatellier et Fils **Director:** M. F. Chatellier, aided by Michel Dufaure **Surface area of vineyard:** 50 hectares (total property 120 hectares) **Average age of vines:** 18 years **Grape production:** 65% Cabernet, 30% Merlot, 5% Verdot **Production:** 250,000 bottles **Local sales:** Tel (56) 88 32 10, **and by mail order** (in France and abroad): Château Dauzac, Labarde, 33460 Margaux **Retail sales**

'The vineyard of Dauzac was renowned from the thirteenth century, as part of the property of the abbey Ste Croix-de-Bordeaux.' It is surprising to find that this *5ᵉ cru classé* of the Labarde commune was already famous in the Middle Ages. This is, however, how it is presented in many of the works which refer to it and in the glossy publicity campaign that its most recent owner, M. Chatellier, offers to amateur wine-lovers. Back in the thirteenth century the poor Benedictine monks of the abbey of Ste Croix were in need of lands for building. They had left things a little late, as the canons of St Seurin, St André and the other large parishes of Bordeaux had divided between themselves the best urban and suburban districts. The politics of evangelical exploitation at St Croix extended still further in Médoc and elsewhere. Two refuges were created at Macau and to the west of Arsac. The property at Macau included the modern property of Dauzac. Small villages were rapidly constructed to house the wandering orders, giving them a scrap of earth to cultivate and a goal in life, that of doing 'good works'.

It was between the years 1220 and 1240 that the first vines appeared at Ludon, Macau and Labarde. At the time these were planted in rich soil and, as such, I believe they had little to do with the celebrity of the wine in question. Little is known of the origins of the Dauzac variety. Its name is probably derived from the Gallo-Roman Davius or Davinius, which is more common in central France. This land may have 109

The grape harvest at La Maqueline at the turn of the century.

been part of the property of Lesparre in the fifteenth century, and the name then changed to Dauzats. It was not until the advent of Compte Jean-Baptiste Lynch, Mayor of Bordeaux at the very beginning of the nineteenth century, that Dauzac appeared as a fine vineyard established on the rockier ground it occupies today. There is no possible doubt that it is entirely thanks to Lynch that Dauzac is today a *cru classé*, even though he sold the property several years before the classification took place. It was bought at this time by a certain Wiebrock who soon unloaded the property in favour of Nathaniel Johnston.

Johnston was an extraordinary innovator in the world of wine. It was he who made the first attempts at spraying the crop to prevent mildew. Dauzac was the scene of his experiments and their success is well known (the use of lime and copper sulphate diluted in water was originally discovered at Ducru-Beaucaillou, but that is another story). Johnston's innovation did not stop there, however, since he was extremely enthusiastic about the *'méthode champenoise'*. Johnston, himself sparkling with ideas, produced as many sparkling wines as possible. He pressed the wines of Dauzac and La Maqueline (an area of rich soil between Labarde and Macau) and, before they were fully fermented, took them across the river and turned them into 'Royal Médoc Mousseux' in his cellars at Bourg-sur-Gironde. In spite of several superb successes in the more classical vinification process, Château Dauzac never achieved its former glory. This was a bad time for the variety, which the Bernat family had no success in improving. The Miailhe family bought up the property in 1964 and partly restored the vineyard, but it was uphill work. An attempt to launch a new label, Dauzac-Lynch, was thwarted by the rival varieties Lynch-Bages, Lynch-Moussas and Pontac-Lynch. The new venture failed and the vineyard changed hands yet again.

The Chatellier family are the current owners of Dauzac. Since 1978 they have worked hard to restore both the vineyard and the property. If Lynch himself were to visit the property he would no doubt be pleased to see that although the vineyard lacks maturity, the scientific experience of Professor Peynaud is rapidly enhancing both the production and reputation of the wine. The greatest advantage to come from the chequered history of the vineyard is that the lands have been left to rest for almost two generations. There are few *crus classés* which have enjoyed such a holiday. And Dauzac is back with a bang.

Desmirail (Château)

3ᵉ cru classé

Main areas: Cantenac and Arsac (formerly Margaux) **Owner:** Lucien Lurton **Steward:** Brigitte Lurton **Maître de chai:** Philippe Peschka **Surface area of vineyard:** 18 hectares (total property 50 hectares) **Average age of vines:** 25 years **Grape production:** 69% Cabernet-Sauvignon, 7% Cabernet-Franc, 23% Merlot 1% Petit-Verdot **Production:** 35,000–70,000 (!) bottles **Retail sales:** All major shippers of Bordeaux

---

'L'élégant Desmirail, dont la trame serrée,
Laisse échapper le feu d'une liqueur ambrée'.
It is more than appropriate to quote Biarnez with regard to this *cru* since he was the grandfather of Robert von Mendelssohn, the owner of Desmirail before the First World War. Robert was the son of a family of Berlin bankers which also produced the famous musician. In this case, however, the 'midsummer-night's dream' turned out to be a nightmare for the kindly German banker, since his lands were confiscated and he never again set foot on his property. In 1923 M. Michel became the owner until the end of the Second World War. He finally sold off small slices of the property and Desmirail ceased to exist as far as wine production was concerned. Paul Zuger bought the château which was constructed in 1860 after the style of Louis XIII. He managed to revive the variety by producing wine from small plots of land on the property.

Originally Desmirail was a small patch of land from the larger Rauzan property presented as a dowry for the wife of M. Desmirail. At the time it was about 14 hectares of good Margalaise vinestock, and M. Desmirail, well satisfied, gave his name to both the young lady and the *cru*. These days things have changed yet again. The name of Château Desmirail still exists and Jean-Claude Zuger has renamed it Marquis d'Alesme-Becker, which was another Margaux *cru classé* without a château name. For several years Desmirail became the second name of Château Palmer. Lucien Lurton finally restored the property, which today occupies 18 hectares as first noted in the 1855 survey.

To consolidate the property Lucien Lurton purchased the buildings of Port-Aubin, which had first been prosperous in the wine trade at the end of the eighteenth century. We must admire M. Lurton for his perseverance and sense of heritage for, without him, Desmirail would probably have completely disappeared. Combining both Oriental philosophy and a Christian conscience, he is a true master of the vine. We must also admire his strong commercial sense which divides his production of Margaux between three different *crus classés* (Château Brane-Cantenac, Château Durfort-Vivens, Château Desmirail) and several secondary varieties, Château Baudry being the second wine of Desmirail.

Desmirail is dead. Long live Desmirail!

Deyrem-Valentin (Château)

cru bourgeois

Main area: Soussans **Owner:** Jean Sorge, who oversees both direction and cultivation **Surface area of vineyard:** 9.2 hectares (total property 13.7 hectares) **Average age of vines:** 30 years **Grape production:** Red: Cabernet-Sauvignon, Merlot, Malbec, Petit-Verdot **Production:** 60,000 bottles **Local sales:** Tel (56) 88 35 70, **and by mail order** (France only): Château Deyrem-Valentin, Soussans, 33460 Margaux **Retail sales:** Several Bordeaux shippers

The vineyard of this good *cru bourgeois* is situated at Marsac, a commune of Soussans, bordering on Lascombes, Malescot and the two Labégorce vineyards. Both Jean Sorge's home and the *chais* are in Soussans. His grandfather, Maurice Blanc, bought this small property in 1928. Deyrem-Valentin is the name of a former owner whose lineage is forgotten but who represented Soussans on the *Conseil cantonal* (the regional council) at Margaux during the First Republic in the last decade of the eighteenth century.

Jean Sorge is personally responsible for the upkeep of his property and, being proficient in all aspects of the work, does so very ably. If his wine can sometimes be a little lacking in body, it is nevertheless remarkable for its bouquet and finesse. This is only to be expected from Marsac, which is well known to be the best area of Soussans. Over the past few years more and more of the wine is bottled on the property.

Dupeyron (Château) ♙ → Canuet

Durfort-Vivens (Château)

2ͤ cru classé

Main area: Margaux **Owner:** Lucien Lurton **Chef de culture:** Yves Camelot **Maître de chai:** Guy Birot **Surface area of vineyard:** 20 hectares (total property 40 hectares) **Average age of vines:** 25 years **Grape production:** 80% Cabernet-Sauvignon, 12% Cabernet-Franc, 8% Merlot **Production:** 90,000 bottles **Local sales:** see Brane-Cantenac, **and by mail order** (France only): Château Durfort-Vivens, 33460 Margaux **Retail sales:** Descaves, Nicolas, Agence Igor (Paris), Moueix, Hédiard

The name of the counts of Durfort de Duras first appear in the history of Margaux towards the middle of the twelfth century. They were a powerful family of landowners in the province of Guyenne, particularly in the what is today Lot-et-Garonne. In 1450 Thomas de Durfort was the uncontested lord of Margaux whose property included the Château de La Mothe (now Château Margaux) and the largest part of the land occupied by the present day commune. Through a series of matrimonial alliances

The ancient tonnellerie *of Durfort-Vivens on the outskirts of Margaux village.*

Durfort also gained possesion of Montalembert. In the seventeenth century the owners of Margaux and Durfort waged a fierce battle of weathercocks, each of them denying to their neighbour the right to fix a weathervane on their roof. At this time Durfort was rejoined with Lascombes.

In 1768 the Marquis de Montalembert divided Durfort between his two nephews, Montbrison and Vivens. The Viscount of Vivens lost no time in ridding himself of his cousin and, following the fashion of the time, he turned his property into a model vineyard: Durfort-Vivens. During his famous visit to Bordeaux in 1787, Thomas 113

Jefferson particularly distinguished this *cru* and placed it at the head of the *'2ᵉ classé'*, a place which was confirmed in the official classification of 1855. A new alliance was subsequently formed between the Viscount of Puységur and a niece of the Vivens family. In 1866, the Puységurs sold Durfort to two well-known wine-growers, Richier and de La Barre. They were the first in the whole of the Médoc region to replace the wooden vine supports by wire and introduce the self-sufficient vineyard. After belonging for a short time to M. Beaucourt and M. Delmée, Durfort became, in 1895, the property of a wealthy Bordeaux businessman, M. G. Delor. It was he who extended both the lands and the buildings to their present size.

Abel Delor sold Château Durfort in 1937 to my father, Pierre Ginestet, administrator of Château Margaux at the time. Following the sale Abel Delor insisted, despite my father's protestations, in accompanying him on his tour of ownership, detailing the inventory of the property and showing him all the nooks and crannies of the buildings. Entering a small cellar attached to the Château my father was astonished to find a large quantity of racked bottles which formed a collection of the best vintages produced by the *cru* over a century. 'But look', said my father, 'you've forgotten to empty this cellar!' 'My good man,' replied Delor, 'I simply couldn't decently let you move in here with an empty cellar!' Fifty years later, the delicacy of this gesture deserves to be recognized. In 1961 my father decided to sell the vineyard and the title to Lucien Lurton, while reserving the house in his name. The joint production of the Margaux and Durfort *crus* had a bad effect on the latter which was treated as a *'2ᵉ vin de Château Margaux'* and not as a *'2ᵉ cru classé de Margaux'*. Apparently inadvertent, the nuance was nevertheless widely felt. On the other hand, Lucien Lurton owned vines at Brane-Cantenac which were part of the Durfort property in 1855, and the Château Durfort-Vivens vineyard is now back in the hands of one owner. Along with those of Rausan, the wines are the most elegant and delicate of all the Margaux *appellation controlée*.

Ferrière (Château)

3ᵉ cru classé

For details see Lascombes

After the fall of Robespierre, Jean Ferrière came back to power and was mayor of Bordeaux in 1795. Among his numerous famous relatives was one Gabriel Ferrière, a landowner at Margaux. The vineyard was kept within the family until 1914, when Henri Ferrière sold it to Armand Feuillerat who was then the owner of Marquis de Terme. Mme Durand, Feuillerat's daughter, made over the running of the property to Alexis Lichine on behalf of the Count of Château Lascombes in 1960. Since then Ferrière has become the younger brother of Lascombes.

Between 10 and 20 barrels are produced each year under the name of Château Ferrière. The château building, situated in the centre of the village facing the new Margaux school, is a fine residence built in the eighteenth-century style.

Fontarney
(Domaine de) ♙
→ Desmirail

♟♟♟♟♟

Gassies du Vieux-Bourg (Château)

♟♟♟♟♟

cru artisan

Main area: Arsac **Owner:** Louis Gassies, who oversees both direction and production **Surface area of vineyard:** 1 hectare (total property 1 hectare) **Average age of vines:** 15 years **Grape production:** Merlot and Cabernet **Production:** 1000 bottles, sold to various retailers **Local sales:** Tel (56) 88 32 38, **and by mail order** (France only): Château Gassies du Vieux-Bourg, Le Bourg, Arsac, 33460 Margaux.

The noble house of Gassies was extremely important in Margaux and the surrounding areas, especially during the sixteenth and seventeenth centuries. The house made a strong local impression with the production of the Château Rauzan-Gassies, a *2ᵉ cru classé*. The modern Château Gassies du Vieux-Bourg, however, has nothing to do with the former Gassies land. This modest vineyard has been passed through the females of the family for the last five generations. After the war, a Mlle Montminoux (member of an old Arsac family) married Louis Gassies from Pauillac. They decided to take upon themselves the responsibility of running the vineyard and, to show his good faith in the venture, Louis Gassies gave it his own name, as had previously the Baron of Brane and the Chevalier of Lascombes. Whether or not he would have done this had his name been Dupont we shall never know.

Louis Gassies sells most of his wine in barrels, reserving only a small amount for bottling on site. I believe that the Crédit Agricole should encourage the ageing and bottling of Margaux wines on the farms of their origin. In this way both the image and the consumer of Margaux wines would benefit.

Giscours (Château)

♟♟♟♟♟

3ᵉ cru classé

Main area: Labarde **Owner:** GFA du Château Giscours **Director:** Pierre Tari **Steward:** Lucien Guillemet **Chef de culture:** J.P. Laduche **Maître de chai:** G. Sérani **Surface area of vineyard:** 80 hectares, of which 70 are in production (total property 267 hectares) **Average age of vines:** 30 years **Grape production:** Red: 70% Cabernet-Sauvignon, 25% Merlot, 3% Cabernet-Franc, 2% Petit-Verdot **Production:** 375,000 bottles **Local sales:** Tel (56) 88 34 02, **and by mail order** (France only): Château Giscours, Labarde, 33460 Margaux **Retail sales:** Société Gilbey de Loudenne, Château Loudenne, 33340 Saint-Yzans-du-Médoc

Aerial view of the impressive Château Giscours.

Château Giscours is the flagship of the Labarde commune: one crosses its lands on entering Margaux from Bordeaux. There is a superb vineyard, practically unbroken, stretching from Arsac in the west to the village of Labarde in the east. The château, surrounded by its lands and splendid park, lies in the middle of a natural clearing. The name itself, Labarde, is of Celtic origin, and means 'singing bird' or more precisely, 'the lark'. This same name is found in the so-called 'Cantelaude' (*lauda* being the Latin for lark) which is found to the south of the property, on the edges of the Labarde, Macau and Arsac communes.

Giscours is probably derived from the Gallo-Roman Giscous or Giscos and served as a pseudonym for the Marquis Claude-Anne de Saint-Simon following his exile to Spain in 1790. The property was confiscated during the Revolution and Giscours was sold, in 1795, to an American, a wine-growing pioneer of the first order. Like many of

its peers, Giscours first made its mark in the nineteenth century. Marc Promis, the Count of Pescatore, and Edouard Cruse were successively in charge of this exceptional cultural entity. The first renovated the vineyard, the second the château, and the third the production buildings. Above all, the distinguished agricultural engineer, M. P. Skavinski, was for almost half a century the roving ambassador of Giscours, dedicating both his scientific and personal skills to enhancing the new-found reputation of the *cru*.

There followed almost half a century of obscurity, during which Giscours fell into disrepair. The Second World War finally sank the flagship which, plundered and abandoned, was finally restored to the worthy hands of Nicolas Tari. Since 1952, through hard work and dedication, he has effected a slow but steady renovation of the property. The vineyard has been progressively replanted and the *chais*, the vats, the 117 model farm and the château have been painstakingly repaired and completely restored. The *cru* has been re-established as worthy of its 1855 classification, and since 1970 Pierre Tari, Nicolas's son, has been his father's second-in-command. He now has the perfect workforce and with their aid has added a resolutely modern flavour to the natural goodness of the *cru*. He is especially good in the role of *porte-parole*, public relations man, press officer, guest of honour at receptions and banquets, globe-trotting gourmet and polo-player. All this has been useful in restoring the reputation of the Giscours wines. Over relatively little time the château has enjoyed the widest press coverage of all the *crus classés*. During this time a battalion of experts, headed by Professor Henri Enjalbert and aided by Jacques Puisais, Pascal Ribéreau-Gayon and Emile Peynaud, have taken a lively interest in the Tari property. They observed, reflected, and advised the Taris to dig a 12 hectare pool to aid natural drainage (already improved in the nineteenth century by the ornamental pools in the park) and to enhance the favourable microclimate. The excavation also permitted the family to reclaim land lost through erosion. At Giscours they are used to digging lakes, raising hills and . . . printing an exclusive magazine, *Giscours Réalité*, which one might take for an extract from *Vogue*. 'Second to none' the Tari family proudly declare is their motto.

Château Giscours, a *3ᵉ cru classé* in 1855, would be difficult to place today. It may be possible that it has achieved its aim of peerless excellence, but that is for the consumer to decide. As for me, I find the Giscours well made and very palatable.

Graveline (Château)

cru artisan

Main area: Arsac **Owner:** René Poujeau, who oversees both direction and production **Surface area of vineyard:** 1 hectare (total property 1.26 hectares) **Average age of vines:** 16 and 13 years **Retail sales:** MM. Gardère-Harambourn SA, quai Jean-Fleuret, 33250 Pauillac

Gravières de Marsac (Château)

→ *Marsac-Séguineau*

Graviers (Château des)

cru artisan

Main area: Arsac **Owner:** M. Durfourg-Landry, who oversees both direction and production **Surface area of vineyard:** 7 hectares (total property 7 hectares) **Average age of vines:** 20 years **Grape production:** Cabernet-Sauvignon and Merlot **Production:** 25,000 bottles **Local sales:** Tel (56) 88 34 73, **and by mail order** (France only): Château des Graviers, Arsac, 33460 Margaux **Retail sales:** Very small amounts

Haut Breton Larigaudière (Château)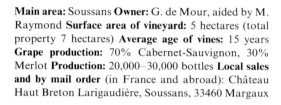

cru bourgeois supérieur

Main area: Soussans **Owner:** G. de Mour, aided by M. Raymond **Surface area of vineyard:** 5 hectares (total property 7 hectares) **Average age of vines:** 15 years **Grape production:** 70% Cabernet-Sauvignon, 30% Merlot **Production:** 20,000–30,000 bottles **Local sales and by mail order** (in France and abroad): Château Haut Breton Larigaudière, Soussans, 33460 Margaux

It is certainly not forbidden for us to declare our personal belief that the old classifications, which were made more than a century ago, could usefully be revised, should the occasion and the necessity arise... Let us consider the Château Haut Breton Larigaudière; bearing in mind that this is a *cru bourgeois* and considering at the same time the harvests there... a carriage, drawn by a fine horse and correctly handled, takes us for a spin around the château. On entering the great court, the carriage circles widely and takes us to the front door. We are immediately surrounded by an enchanting group of children, with dark velvety eyes, curly hair and well-tanned faces. What a wonderful welcome to this beautiful area! Everyone seems happy and contented, from the smiling baby at his mother's breast, to the beautiful

The harvest at Haut Breton Larigaudière drawn by Bertall in 1877.

elegant young women, from the voluptuous mothers to the no less attractive aunts... 'Welcome, welcome,' declares the mistress of the house, 'make yourselves at home. My dear,' she adds to her husband, 'everything is ready, and tomorrow we harvest...' Early the next day, the men and women are hard at work; the carts, drawn by sturdy horses, are waiting in driveways and the whole operation takes place beneath the vigilant eye of the master and mistress. Just as in the greatest châteaux, the grapes are picked and pressed and the juice and must carried to the vats. As evening falls the legendary beef soup with cabbage is prepared by the mistress herself in large cooking pots. As soon as this meal is finished, everyone dances to the sound of the flageolet and the violin, before retiring ready to begin again the next day.

These extracts from *La Vigne* by Bertall (Paris, 1878) colourfully depict the harvests of the time at Haut Breton Larigaudière. The then owner, M. Landau, was careful to ensure that his product was worthy 'of its rather more advantageously classified compatriots'. In 1870, Haut Breton was producing about 30 *tonneaux* a year. Twenty years later, the figure had risen to 80 but by the beginning of the twentieth century it had dropped to 40, finally falling as low as 10 at the end of the war and to zero in the 1960s. During the last century the property changed hands five times, and as such is a perfect example of the rise and fall of the Médoc *crus*, which mirror the good or bad treatment they receive. The château has been restored since 1964 by the house of G. de Mour et Fils on 5 hectares of the former property. Since 1980 the vineyard has begun once more to demonstrate its capacity for producing excellent wine. There is now also a restaurant serving local cuisine for visitors to the château.

Hautes Graves (Château)

cru artisan

Main area: Soussans **Owner:** Marcel Eyquem (33480 Avensan), who has cultivated this tiny vineyard himself for almost forty years. It came to him through marriage. I am not too sure how he disposes of his produce, but it is difficult to believe that he manages to drink it all himself. **Surface area of vineyard:** 3 hectares **Average age of vines:** 15 years

Haut-Tayac (Château)

cru bourgeois

Main area: Soussans **Owners:** Christian and Viviane Saux **Director:** Christian Saux, who oversees both direction and production **Surface area of vineyard:** 10 hectares (total property 60 hectares) **Average age of vines:** 20 years **Grape production:** Cabernet and Merlot **Production:** 85% is bottled on site (approximately 50,000 bottles) **Local sales:** Tel (56) 88 34 29, **and by mail order** (in France and abroad): Château Haut-Tayac, Tayac, Soussans, 33460 Margaux **Retail sales**

The Margaux appellation runs along the river and its central axis, drawn from the south-east to the north-west, runs from Labarde to Tayac. This village, belonging to the Soussans commune, was previously a ragged collection of about twenty small-holders, each working a tiny individual vineyard. The majority of these have now disappeared and this gravelly plateau, formed of low hillocks, is nowadays divided into two properties. The Château Haut-Tayac is one of them, and Christian and Viviane Saux are the young, dynamic owners of this 10 hectare vineyard. The property has been in the family of Viviane Saux, née Blanc, for five generations.

The Haut-Tayac wine is both powerful and tannic. Although a little rough when young, it improves in the cask. Its fine constitution and local accent do not detract from the intrinsic finesse which one expects in a Margaux *cru bourgeois*.

Issan (Château d')

3e cru classé

Main area: Cantenac **Owner:** Société civile du Château d'Issan–G.F.A., 33460 Margaux, Tel (56) 88 73 93 **President:** Mme Emmanuel Cruse **Director:** Lionel Cruse **Chef de culture and maître de chai:** M. Arnaudin **Surface area of vineyard:** 32 hectares (total property 120 hectares) **Average age of vines:** 20 years **Grape production:** Red: 75% Cabernet-Sauvignon, 25% Merlot **Production:** 120,000 bottles **Retail sales:** All the major wine shippers of Bordeaux

In the fourteenth century the Margaux region was dominated by two properties, La Mothe-Margaux and La Mothe-Cantenac. The first became Château Margaux, the second Château d'Issan. These two properties are quite similar as regards their layout, their proximity to the river and their network of wide irrigation canals, which previously were used to transport foodstuffs, and, prior to that, as protection for country homes. In this way Issan, along with Château Margaux, is the oldest property in the country and, as it is today, the château is one of the oldest in the whole Médoc region.

In the fifteenth century it was called Théobon, which is probably of Gallo-Roman origin. At that time the property was much larger that it is today and covered almost all the area of the Cantenac commune. The families de Mayrac, de Ségur, de Salignac, de La Vergne were all in turn owners of Théobon until the Chevalier Pierre d'Essenault, a counsellor in the parliament of Bordeaux, took possession of the lands. It was he who demolished the old fortified château and, at the beginning of the seventeenth century, built the fine house which still stands today. It is from him that the present-day Issan takes its name. A century later, the houses of Foix de Candale and de Castelnau were part-owners in both the lands and the Château d'Issan. At this time the *cru* was widely known under the name of Candale, but with the Revolution the property was confiscated and turned over to citizen Castelnau. After his wife had quarrelled with the local administration in Margaux, the property was divided and sold at public auction. It was bought in 1794 by Etienne Veissière, who took over farming the former Maison Candale. This career was cut short when, following his failure to pay taxes, all his wines were confiscated by the Receiver.

At the beginning of the nineteenth century Issan was often named as the best Cantenac wine and was owned in succession by the Duluc family (who also gave their name to the Château Branaire wine in Saint Julien), the Blanchy family, and the Roy family. Its classification in 1855 as a *3^e cru* in no way reflected its fine reputation over the two previous centuries. It required a man of great courage like Emmanuel Cruse, who, after the last war, bought the property which consisted of a rundown vineyard, a dilapidated château, and a brand name which, for over fifty years, had been in decline. He made slow but steady progress and, over a considerable period of time, restored the Château d'Issan to its former glory.

The property had not altogether lost its potential and the 32 hectares which form the vineyard have been replanted over a twenty-year span. During this time, the buildings were re-styled and the château completely restored in the austere style of Louis XIII. After the death of her husband Mme Emmanuel Cruse brought her own personal contribution to Issan. It has now become one of the high spots of 'Mai de Bordeaux', an annual function combining international musicians and the oldest families of Bordeaux. Lionel Cruse, Emmanuel's son, has taken charge of the administration of the property and faithfully upholds the work begun by his father.

When the English were chased from Médoc in 1451 by Dunois, they loaded their

The Château d'Issan is one of the most beautiful houses in the Margaux region.

ships with all the best wines of Théobon. Three centuries later the Prince of Wales declared that his wine cellar contained wines from Candale. Two centuries after that the Emperor Franz Joseph of Austria named Issan as his favourite wine. Obviously these were all people of taste. The 1900 vintage is certainly one of the best wines I have ever tasted. *Regum Mensis Arisque Deorum* (for the table of kings and the altar of the gods) runs the motto. Drinking Issan, one can be both king and god.

Kirwan (Château)

Main area: Cantenac **Owner:** Shröder & Schÿler et Cie **Director:** J. H. Schÿler **Chef de culture:** L. Demezzo **Oenologist:** Latapy **Surface area of vineyard:** 31 hectares (total property 65 hectares) **Average age of vines:** 18 years **Grape production:** 40% Cabernet-Sauvignon, 30% Merlot, 20% Cabernet-Franc, 10% Petit-Verdot **Production:** 160,000 bottles **Mail order:** Château Kirwan, Cantenac, 33460 Margaux **Retail sales:** Schröder & Schÿler et Cie, 97 quai des Chartrons, 33300 Bordeaux

3ᵉ cru classé

Château Kirwan, a delightful gentleman's residence of the nineteenth century.

124

'Château Kirwan is certainly the greatest of the *troisième crus*. The fortunate owner of this vineyard exhibits the gracious hospitality one would expect from the noble wine-growers of la Gironde and his *chais* are of the finest quality.' In 1865 Dr Aussel (in *La Gironde à vol d'oiseau*) had good reason to praise Kirwan and the hospitality of Camille Godard, the affable, refined country gentleman who himself designed the park for his château before becoming Mayor of Bordeaux. He acquired this property from a rich businessman call Schryver. It is fitting that the town of Bordeaux should name one of its streets after the man who died at Kirwan in 1881, leaving his brother, Adolphe Godard, owner until he himself died in 1895. It was then that the well-known firm of Schröder & Schÿler et Cie obtained exclusive rights to retail the wines produced at Château Kirwan. In 1904 the municipality of Bordeaux, understanding little of wine-growing, handed over the property to Daniel and Georges Guestier. The firm of Schröder & Schÿler had widely distributed the Kirwan wines, sometimes with no indication of the *cru*, and had sold them as a purely commercial product, with no sign of their true origin or vintage. This situation was in part remedied when Alfred Schÿler married the daughter of Daniel Guestier. The marriage was a success and produced lots of fine little Kirwans. When Daniel died, in 1924, Schröder and Schÿler bought the property so that there could be no repetition of the previous mismanagement.

Kirwan is a family name of Celtic origin which is found in the county of Galway in Ireland. A young Kirwan married the daughter of Sir John Collingwood who in 1760 had bought the largest part of the lands of Reynard de La Salle (Château Kirwan was previously called La Salle and it was Camille Godard who united the property by purchasing land from one of La Salle's heirs). Monarchist, pro-clergy, liberal and fiercely patriotic, the previous Kirwan was guillotined during the Revolution, leaving behind a large family to quarrel over the inheritance. I discovered this description of Marc Kirwan, then aged 64, in a document dating from 1799: 'He was five foot three inches tall, with blond hair and eyebrows. He had blue eyes, a long nose, medium-sized mouth and a round chin. His forehead rose high from an oval face and he was the the foremost businessman in Bordeaux.' Jean-Henri Schÿler, a direct descendant of the Schÿler who founded the famous company with Jacques Schröder in 1739, is the current director of the Société de Commerce et du Château Kirwan. He is ably assisted in this role by his wife Christine Krug, a member of the famous Champagne family.

The Kirwan property is situated on a vast inclined plain, typical of the Cantenac commune. The sandy, gravelly soil is kept well drained because of the thin, clayey subsoil. These characteristics produce very powerful concentrated wines which are at the same time tannic and 'thick'. They become more subtle with age, losing the aggression of their youth and taking on the traditional delicacy of the Margaux wines. Each year part of the store of wine casks is renewed in oak wood so that the freshness is preserved along with the fine bouquet. In spite of its susceptibility to wet weather, Château Kirwan has had marvellous success in the vintage years, especially when the Merlot grapes which form one-third of the vineyard are harvested in perfect condition.

Labégorce (Château)

cru bourgeois supérieur

Main area: Margaux **Owner:** Jean-Robert Condom **Director:** Jean-Robert Condom **Chef de culture:** Paul Richard **Maître de chai:** Michael Duboscq **Surface area of vineyard:** 29.18 hectares (total property 68 hectares) **Average age of vines:** 20 years **Grape production:** 55% Cabernet-Sauvignon, 40% Merlot, 5% Cabernet-Franc **Production:** 130,000 bottles **Local sales:** Tel (56) 88 79 32, **and by mail order:** Château Labégorce, 33460 Margaux **Retail sales:** Mainly through the Maison Dourthe Frères, quai de Bacalan, Bordeaux

On 31 August 1865 M. Fortuné Beaucourt invested 224,000 gold francs in the purchase of Labégorce from the law court of Bordeaux. This was ten years after the classification and a century after the peak of production in the Margaux vineyards. Although it was

Situated between Margaux and Soussans, Labégorce is surrounded by vineyards.

too late for it to become a *cru classé*, Fortuné Beaucourt turned Labégorce into the best *cru bourgeois supérieur* of the Margaux commune. Prior to this purchase the history of the property is somewhat complicated. Through investigation I discovered that the said Labégorce was 'acquired' in 1793 from the rich family de Mons at Soussans by citizen Weltener. He lost no time in selling the property to one Pierre Capelle who, in turn, resold to M. Vastapani. But why on earth would Vastapani continue to call his *cru* Weltener? Possibly because of his rivalry with Gorse's widow, who was living in the same area. Perhaps one day we shall fully understand the significance of this little human drama. Gorse (or Gorce) is a very old Guyenne name which was used throughout Médoc in the Middle Ages (it was of course the former name of Brane-

Cantenac). There have been several families named Gorse living in Margaux and the neighbouring communes for centuries and nothing remains of the original 'abbé Gorse' except the vineyard to which it gave its name.

Once installed as the new owner of Labégorce, Fortuné Beaucourt made great progress in renovating the *cru's* production. Little liked because of his strong personality and severe character, he concentrated on improving the reputation of his wine. He was twice mayor of Margaux between 1870 and 1900 and took a great interest in the collective welfare of the wine producers in his commune (in particular ensuring that the people living by the river helped drain the vineyards by cleaning out the ditches). It was he who had the château built after plans prepared by Corcelles, a famous architect of the time. It was also through his influence that the first telephone line was connected between Bordeaux and Pauillac. In 1918 Labégorce was bought by the Rooryck family, who maintained the reputation of the *cru* and sold the property in 1965 to M. and Mme Robert Condom. M. Condom was previously involved in advertising and came to the Médoc as a place of peaceful retirement. He was passionately interested in his vineyard and its produce and so took easily to his new profession, bringing a breath of fresh air to the property. Shortly after his arrival, however, he died before fully enjoying the fulfilment of his lifetime's ambition. His wife dedicated herself to the task at hand, but she also died not long afterwards. Their son, Jean-Robert Condom, the young owner of Labégorce, must now prove himself worthy of the lineage of the *'grands bourgeois supérieurs'*. Professor Peynaud and an experienced team of dedicated helpers are there to guarantee the continuing quality of the wine.

Labégorce Zédé (Château)

cru bourgeois

Main areas: Soussans and Margaux **Owner:** G.F.A. Labégorce Zédé **Director and chef de culture:** Luc Thienpont **Maître de chai:** Jean Bergamin **Surface area of vineyard:** 25 hectares (total property 42 hectares) **Average age of vines:** 25 years **Grape production:** 50% Cabernet-Sauvignon, 35% Merlot, 10% Cabernet-Franc, 5% Petit-Verdot **Production:** 120,000 bottles **Local sales:** Tel (56) 89 71 31 **Retail sales:** Mainly through Bordeaux retailers

At the end of the nineteenth century two well-known 'Zs' appeared on the military scene in Europe: Ferdinand von Zeppelin arrived by air, Gustave Zédé preferring the submarine. This latter was one of the five children of Pierre Zédé, an appeal judge in the state court, and owner of an important part of the Labégorce property, divided during the Revolution. Gustave Zédé has bequeathed his name to naval history through his torpedo boat, *Le Gymnote*, lauched in 1888. He was the younger brother of Admiral Hyppolyte Zédé, who directed the division of the property 'Labégorce bis' until 1891, when he bought back the shares of his family to assume complete control. The *cru* has since then been known as Labégorce-Zédé and has had an impressive career. In 1931 the Zédé heirs sold the property to their former steward, Pierre Eyrin. The property then passed through the hands of six different owners until in 1961 Jean Battesti, the former president of the Constantine Chamber of Commerce, settled there with his family. Nowadays, and since 1979, it is the young Luc Thienpont and his wife who tend the GFA du Château Labégorce Zédé. Thienpont is a name well known in

The crus bourgeois of Margaux are well represented by Labégorce-Zédé.

the world of wine, notably through its connection with the Vieux Château-Certan at Pomerol. Luc Thienpont has quickly taken root in this patch of Margaux soil, like the best of the Petit-Verdot. He produces well-balanced wines which are distributed by all the main shippers of Bordeaux.

Labory de Tayac (Ch.) 🕯 → Tayac   ♟♟♟♟♟

La Coste (Château) 🕯   ♟♟♟♟♟

→ Paveil de Luze

La Galiane (Château)   ♟♟♟♟♟

cru 1er artisan

Main area: Soussans **Owners:** René and Jeanne Renon, who oversee both direction and production **Surface area of vineyard:** Approximately 4.5 hectares (total property 8 hectares) **Average age of vines:** 60–75 years **Grape production:** 50% Merlot, 50% Cabernet **Production:** 20,000 bottles **Local sales:** Tel (56) 88 35 27, **and by mail order:** Château La Galiane, Soussans, 33460 Margaux

At the time when the English were harvesting the grape crop of Aquitaine, a young and brilliant general named Galiane was commander-in-chief of the English troops engaged in the Médoc region during the Hundred Years War. Galiane certainly did not lack a place to sleep, since he was equally at home in every fort in Médoc. For relaxation, however, he needed something rather more welcoming than the garrisons and so established a *pied à terre* at Soussans for his lighter hours. This place was for many years know as 'à Galiane' and gradually as La Galiane.

Nowadays La Galiane is home for the Renon family. The property came to them through Mme Renon, née Miquau, but not, however, the Miquaus of Margaux nor the Miquaus of Bas-Médoc. She is a descendant of the Miquaus of Soussans who twice monthly attended the fair at Moulis in a two-horse carriage. On hearing the sound of their approach, everyone turned their back on the church of Moulis to see them arrive on the highway: 'Look, here come the Miquaus of Soussans!'

Jeannette and René Renon at La Galiane.

Some ten years ago I lunched at La Galiane. After aperitifs and some light snacks, we progressed to more serious eating. A series of *hors d'oeuvres*, slices of cold pork, a fish dish, a rich salmi of duck, all washed down with the best wines. After four and a half hours of this, we were more than well fed. It was at this moment that Jeannette Renon came out of the kitchen, carrying a leg of lamb with mushrooms of a size that defied description. On behalf of all the guests who begged for mercy, I proposed to Jeannette that this was really too much. She put down the enormous dish of meat, put her hands on her hips and cried indignantly: 'What? Do you think I'd let you leave hungry?' We finally got up from the table at seven in the evening, having drunk two more magnums of 1947 La Galiane.

La Gombeaude (Château) ⚱ → *Lascombes*

La Gurgue (Château)

🍷🍷🍷🍷🍷

cru bourgeois supérieur

Main area: Margaux **Owners:** Société Bernard Taillan and Société Chantovent **Manager and director:** Mme Villars **Steward:** M. Conroy **Maître de chai:** M. Raspaud **Surface area of vineyard:** 12.5 hectares (total property 18.5 hectares) **Average age of vines:** 30 years **Grape production:** Red: 70% Cabernet-Sauvignon, 30% Merlot and Noir de Pressac **Production:** 60,000 bottles **Mail order:** Château Chasse-Spleen, 33380 Moulis **Retail sales:** Hédiard, D'Arfeuille, Ph. Delestrie, Duclot, Delperrier, Ginestet

This château is one of the best-known *bourgeois supérieurs* of Margaux. It has long been placed among the three or four *crus* following the group of *crus classés* in the same commune. In 1791 the banker Peixotto bought the vines from the Margaux priory and added them to his property called La Gurgue (which means the small round bump). La Gurgue is, along with Desmirail, the next-door neighbour to the west of Château Margaux. Two former mayors of Margaux, Lanoire and Lavandier, were owners of the property before the Société civile administered by Mme Horrière sold the vineyard in 1978 to the Sociétés Bernard Taillan and Chantovent. We can be quite confident that, tended by Mme Villars, this *cru* will give full satisfaction to its new owners and we can live in hope that this will be accompanied by the highest quality wines.

L'Aiguillette (Clos de)

cru artisan

Main area: Soussans **Owner:** A. Corporeau. This tiny vineyard takes its name from the narrow, pointed strip of land near Marsac. The soil is excellent. The wine produced by the Corporeau-Frette family is not available commercially. **Surface area of property:** 0.6 hectares **Grape production:** 1/3 Merlot, 1/3 Cabernet-Sauvignon, 1/3 Cabernet-Franc, with a small amount of Petit-Verdot and Malbec

L'Amiral (Ch. de) ♗ → Labégorce-Zédé

La Rose Maucaillou (Domaine)

cru artisan

Main area: Soussans **Owner:** Albert Maugey, who oversees both direction and production **Surface area of vineyard:** 6 hectares (total property 20 hectares) **Average age of vines:** 18 years **Grape production:** Traditional **Production:** 12,000 bottles and approximately 25 tonneaux **Local sales:** Tel (56) 58 21 29, **and by mail order** (in France and abroad): M. Maugey, Château Semonlon, 33480 Avensan

Albert Maugey is better known as the owner of Avensan, where he produces the Château Semonlon wines of the Haut-Médoc appellation. He also produces some good wines at Soussans (see Château Vallière with regard to the label).

Larruau (Château)

cru 'remarquable'

Main area: Margaux **Owner:** Bernard Chateau, who oversees both direction and production **Surface area of vineyard:** 3 hectares (total property 5 hectares) **Average age of vines:** 15 years **Grape production:** Red: 2/3 Cabernet-Sauvignon, 1/3 Merlot **Production:** 12,000 bottles **Local sales:** Tel (56) 88 35 50, **and by mail order:** Château Larruau, 4 rue de La Trémoille, 33460 Margaux **Retail sales**

Augustin Dubignon-Talbot was the local tax assessor for the Margaux district, in the fourth year of the Republic (1796). The château of the same name had been classified a 3e *cru classé* in 1855. With Augustin's death, two new varieties bearing the name of Dubignon were created, one named Philippe, the other G. Martial, later Marcelin. In 1865 the Fourcade family took over the Philippe Dubignon name, adding it to their existing vineyard of St-Exupéry, Malescot, La Colonie, and Prévôt de Lacroix. By the end of the century Malescot-St-Exupéry, a 3e *cru classé* including Dubignon's interest, was the most important vineyard in Margaux apart from the château itself.

During this period M. Veron-Réville was living in the Château Dubignon-Talbot, producing 5–8 *tonneaux* of wine a year on the remaining land. In 1904 Pierre Mellet bought the micro-*cru* and increased production to more than 20 *tonneaux*. In 1960 Jean Cordier, the owner of Château Talbot at St-Julien, bought up the vines and sold them to Château Margaux and Malescot, effectively wiping out the variety.

Since then, the young Bernard Chateau has, on a vineyard of only 3 hectares, created a variety named Larruau after the site of the former Château Dubignon-Talbot. The house is one of the most charming in the village, and the wine, Château Larruau, produced by Bernard Château is exceptional. Although the vineyard is only

Bernard Chateau in his vineyard.

15 years old, it seems on tasting the wine at least twice that age. In my opinion it is the best combination of quality and price available in Margaux.

Lascombes (Château)

2e cru classé

Main area: Margaux **Owner:** La Société du Château Lascombes, belonging to SA Lichine, part of the English Bass group **Director:** Alain Maurel **Steward:** Claude Gobinau **Chef de culture:** Jean-Pierre Sougnoux **Maître de chai:** Robert Dupuy **Surface area of vineyard:** 94 hectares (total property 130 hectares) **Average age of vines:** 69% between 5 and 30 years **Grape production:** 63% Cabernet, 33% Merlot, 3% Petit-Verdot, 1% Cot **Production:** 250,000–300,000 bottles **Local sales:** Tel (56) 88 70 66, **and by mail order:** Société du Château Lascombes, 33460 Margaux **Retail sales:** Alexis Lichine et Cie, 109 rue Achard, 33300 Bordeaux

During the fifties Alexis Lichine brought French wines to the attention of the American public, with particular emphasis on the *grand crus* of Bordeaux. A man of taste and sensibility, he breathed new life into the Médoc, and Margaux was the first beneficiary of his public relations exercise. Not content merely with attracting the attention of the press and importers and distributors, he met the rich families of New York, New England and California, helping them set up their own wine cellars and teaching them how to serve and taste wine – in short, how to use their knowledge of wine to improve their public and private standing.

Lascombes is one of the most popular places for tourists in Margaux.

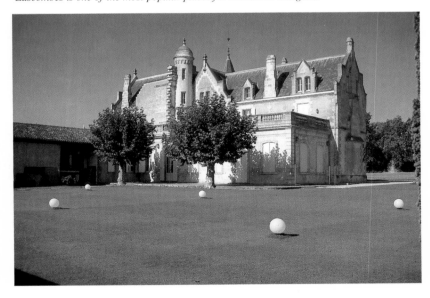

133

Fermentation in open-air vats at Château Lascombes.

Acting on behalf of Château Lascombes, he managed to persuade David Rockefeller to come to Margaux. Rockefeller asked Pierre Ginestet for advice regarding the business and was told: 'Participation in a vineyard will not make you any richer, but it is one of those rare investments which will always bring dividends.' It was thus, in 1952, that a group of rich Americans under the leadership of Alexis Lichine bought Château Lascombes. This was the real beginning of the extraordinary 'wine-man show' of Lichine who was to become a 'pape du vin'.

Lascombes, named after the Chevalier de Lascombes, born in 1625, was originally linked with the house of Durfort-Duras. Classified as a *2ᵉ cru* in 1855, it belonged to the master of the bar, Chaix d'Est-Ange, at the end of the last century. This was the man who, under Napoleon III, defended France against Egypt in the Suez Canal hearings. The modern château, with its unassuming Anglo-baroque style, dates from this time. When Chaix d'Est-Ange died the vineyard was split up into pieces by the neighbouring owners. It was partially restored in the twenties by my grandfather and my father who subsequently sold it to a Société civile, which did little to enhance its reputation. During the last war it was the headquarters of the Canadian general Brutinel, chief adviser to the Allied Armies for the south-west of France and Spain. A well-known tactician, General Brutinel predicted the invasion of 1944 two years in advance. Under the direction of Alexis Lichine, Lascombes was quickly restored and production increased tenfold over the next twenty years. The enlarged *chais* are today among the biggest in Margaux.

In 1971 Château Lascombes was sold to the English company Bass-Charrington, which had previously bought Alexis Lichine's business in Bordeaux. The general direction of the vineyard is now the responsibility of Alain Maurel, son of an old Bordeaux family. The whole place now has a New World style to it: with its Hollywood swimming pool, varnished barrels and stainless steel open-air vats it has the distinct air of a great Californian winery. All available new technology is laid on for the well-run vineyard, though this can sometimes lead to over-production. The vines do not often stick to the 4 metre-high limit along the roadside, set to allow vineyard tractors to turn round.

Thanks to Alexis Lichine and his friends, and to the powerful British company which is the present owner, Château Lascombes is a fine property of which the Margaux commune can be justifiably proud. A huge reception room in front of the *chais* containing the latest vintage allows Lascombes to welcome large groups of visitors from all over the world. I think it only fair to allow Alexis Lichine the last word on his former property: 'Château Lascombes has a consummate finesse. The bouquet is light and hard to classify, underlining the feminine qualities of the wines of the Médoc region which, according to some, are reminiscent of violets. It ages well and quickly yet has a long youthful life.' (*Encyclopédie des vins et des alcools*, Paris, 1980)

La Tour de Bessan (Château)

Main area: Soussans **Owner:** Lucien Lurton **Maître de chai:** M. Birot **Surface area of vineyard:** 21 hectares (total property 40 hectares) **Average age of vines:** 15 years **Grape production:** 90% Cabernet-Sauvignon, 10% Merlot **Production:** 80,000–100,000 bottles **Retail sales:** Among others, the Société de distribution des vins fins, 20 rue Ferrère, 33000 Bordeaux

The tower of Bessan no longer exists beside the flow of La Louise in the Soussans commune. In the fifteenth century the English had built many of these watchtowers throughout the Médoc region. During the reign of Charles VII it was no longer in use except as a support for the ivy, a resting place for the birds, shelter for poachers and a refuge for lovers who, over the centuries, covered the walls with graffiti. As for the château, it has never really existed as an actual building, but it is well known that in Bordeaux, as in Spain, châteaux are often built in spirit rather than in substance. It was in such a spirit that Lucien Lurton constructed a vineyard on the name of La Tour de Bessan. This new variety allowed him to diversify his interests in the production of Margaux appellation wines. Until quite recently, La Tour de Bessan was used to designate the wines of Château La Tour-de-Mons. La Tour de Bessan produces light, gently fruity wines which allow one to drink a Lurton Margaux at dinner without great expense.

La Tour-de-Mons (Château)

cru bourgeois supérieur

Main area: Soussans **Owner:** Indivision Clauzel-Binaud **Director and steward:** Bertrand Clauzel **Chef de culture and maître de chai:** Christian Clauzel **Surface area of vineyard:** 30 hectares (total property 100 hectares) **Average age of vines:** 25 years **Grape production:** 45% Cabernet-Sauvignon, 40% Merlot, 10% Cabernet-Franc, 5% Petit-Verdot **Production:** 120,000 bottles **Local sales:** Tel (56) 88 33 03, **and by mail order:** (France only): Château La Tour-de-Mons, Soussans, 33460 Margaux **Retail sales:** In Bordeaux

Two centuries before Columbus's discovery of America, Jehan de Colomb discovered the Médoc and decided to live there. He settled at Soussans in 1289 during the first economic boom in Bordeaux, due to the presence of the English who encouraged the townspeople to develop viticulture in Guyenne. The greatest families at that time were the Bégueys, the Manadeys, the Salters and the Colombs, who built the Tour-de-Mons. This ancient pile, the oldest in the country, has been rebuilt on several occasions but in spite of this the foundations remain firmly in the thirteenth century. The land, the vineyard and the château are an authentic Margaux antiquity. The Tour-de-Mons was, until the Revolution, the most important 'maison' in Soussans. It is certainly without parallel in that it was passed through the family, without trouble, until the old order ended with the emigration of part of the family; this took away three-quarters of the land which had previously stretched unbroken from Bessan to Labégorce.

Clauzel-Binaud are the latest owners of the property, and it is now administered by Bertrand Clauzel, former mayor of Soussans, and his son Christian, an experienced wine-grower. Their grandfather Dubos was the legendary wine-maker of Cantemerle and La Tour-de-Mons. The memory of his extraordinary vintages still brings tears to

Bertrand Clauzel at La Tour-de-Mons.

the eyes of the older wine tasters. I myself recall a blind tasting of 1953 wines, where La Tour-de-Mons was secretly placed among a dozen *crus classés*. It outclassed all of them and its richness and depth were such that no one could place it. In fact, the wines of La Tour-de-Mons have a particular personality which distinguishes them from the majority of Margaux. They are often taken for Pauillacs and sometimes for Pomerols or Graves. But, above all, they are renowned for the pleasure they bring to the true wine-lover. The price is comparable to that of the *crus classés* and fully justified by the fidelity of its buyers.

La Tourelle (Clos de) 🍶

→ Monbrison

Les Baraillots (Château)

cru artisan

Main area: Margaux **Owner:** Michel Brunet, who oversees both production and direction **Surface area of vineyard:** 4.8 hectares (total property 24 hectares) **Average age of vines:** 20 years **Grape production:** Cabernets, Merlots and Verdots **Production:** 25,000 bottles **Local sales:** Tel (56) 88 33 56, **and by mail order:** Château Les Baraillots, 2 rue Corneillan, 33460 Margaux **Retail sales:** A small amount annually

Michel Brunet and his family, along with their grandmother who is soon to be a hundred years old, live on their 24 hectares, one-fifth of which comprises the vineyard, the rest of the land being dedicated to animal breeding. The vineyard, divided into two main areas, was gradually obtained from Palmer and Durfort in 1928 and 1933. They are made up of permeable gravelly soil which allows them to be worked in traditional style. The wine-making process is truly classical; the ageing likewise. The whole production is taken seriously.

In Médoc dialect *barrail* or *barralhe* is the name given to cloisters, but more generally to a bank of land showing the boundary of personal property or serving as a dike along a ditch. The small hillocks of Château Les Baraillots divide the property from the surrounding *crus classés*, it being one of the rare *crus artisans* of Margaux-Margaux. The wine is firm, tannic and full of vigour. It is a great pity that it is always sold and drunk far too soon.

M. Michel Brunet.

137

Les Graves du Sol (Château)

Main area: Arsac **Owner:** Jacques Bosc, who oversees both direction and production **Surface area of vineyard:** 1.67 hectares **Average age of vines:** 12 years **Grape production:** Red: 20% Merlot, 80% Cabernet-Sauvignon **Production:** Approximately 9 *tonneaux* sold through retail outlets

The population of the Arsac commune has quadrupled over the last twenty years as a large part of its area was sold to housing developers. The gravel extraction contractors having also made large inroads into the area, the vineyards have been in a steady decline since the First World War. Pine forests and oak copses cover a large area, and only a small space is now dedicated to wine growing, and that is surrounded by five housing estates and two gravel pits.

Jacques Bosc was born in Arsac, and his small vineyard is firmly rooted in the gravel and under the sun of his homeland. The wine has no particular label and is, unfortunately, sold as generic Margaux on the Bordeaux market.

Les Gravières (Château) ⚲ →Tayac

Ligondras (Château)

cru 1er artisan

Main area: Arsac **Owner:** Pierre Augeau, who oversees both direction and production **Surface area of vineyard:** 7 hectares (total property 21 hectares) **Average age of vines:** 30 years **Grape production:** Red **Production:** 35,000 bottles **Local sales:** Tel (56) 88 31 43, **and by mail order** (in France and abroad): Château Ligondras, Arsac, 33460 Margaux **Retail sales**

In the Arsac commune, half way along the road from the town to Brane, is a fine plateau of sandy fields. The vines are predominantly Cabernets which produce a good solid wine with plenty of colour and body. Pierre Augeau inherited this property, which was once part of the Château Vincent at Issan in Cantenac, from his father. The family home at Château Ligondras is typical of Médoc architecture at the end of the last century in spite of the recent extensions which are clearly out of character. Visitors are always welcome at Ligondras and if the owner is not at home, try looking in the vineyard or the *chai*. Like all careful managers M. Augeau keeps an eye on everything.

Loyac (Château) ⚲

→ Malescot Saint-Exupéry

Traditional Bordeaux casks at Château Ligondras.

Malescot Saint-Exupéry (Château)

3e cru classé

Main area: Margaux **Owner:** Roger Zuger **Chef de culture:** Jean-Claude Durand **Maître de chai:** Jean-François Miquau **Surface area of vineyard:** 34 hectares (total property 58 hectares) **Average age of vines:** 35 years **Grape production:** Red: 50% Cabernet-Sauvignon, 35% Merlot, 10% Cabernet-Franc, 5% Petit-Verdot **Production:** 180,000 bottles **Local sales:** Tel (56) 88 70 68, **and by mail order** (France only): Château Malescot Saint-Exupéry, 33460 Margaux **Retail sales:** Exclusive shippers in each country

Roger and Nicole Zuger have brought new life to Malescot Saint-Exupéry.

Roger Zuger has succeeded both his father and mine as president of the Syndicat viticole de l'Appellation Margaux. This new syndicate was created to replace the original Syndicat des Vignobles de Margaux, founded in 1920 before Margaux had its own appellation. At that time, Malescot Saint-Exupéry was owned by the English firm of W. H. Chaplin and Company Limited, who specialized in the importation of Australian wines. Since the beginning of the nineteenth century, however, Malescot is one of the Médoc varieties which has most often changed hands. In 1827, Count Jean-Baptiste de Saint-Exupéry added his name to that of Malescot (who was the state prosecutor in the seventeenth-century Bordeaux parliament) and at the same time added a quantity of vines to the property taken from the surrounding areas of La Colonie and Loyac. He was succeeded by Fourcade in 1853, who continued the expansion by adding Dubignon (Philippe), Prévôt de Lacroix and several other scattered pieces of land. This is today what one might modestly describe as 'careful change' . . . From 1850 to 1865 the production of Malescot Saint-Exupéry was increased from 75 to 200 *tonneaux* and, over a ten-year period, 500,000 feet of vines were planted. The field-work was carried out by a team including fourteen oxen and six horses, and harvesting the crop required the services of nearly 300 people.

The estate passed through the hands of ten different owners in less than a century and a half until the château was purchased, on 1 June 1955, by Paul Zuger. The impressive property had been reduced to 7 hectares of ailing vines, dilapidated out-buildings, broken-down equipment and a name whose reputation had suffered badly. In twenty-five years, Paul Zuger and his son Roger have rebuilt the vineyard to a size commensurate with that of a *cru classé*. The roofs have been repaired, the *chais* remodelled, and a new building for conditioning and stocking is almost complete. Roger Zuger, who is passionately interested in heraldry, has had the Saint-Exupéry coat of arms re-engraved in gold on the Malescot label. It consists of lions rampant to one side and on the other a crown above a flying banner with the proud motto *Semper ad altum.*

The highs and lows of a *cru classé* over the centuries are exemplified in the colourful history of Château Malescot. One can trace a link between the unpredictability of the Médoc climate and the destiny of the *grands crus*, and one can also judge the 1855 classification, which granted five classes of privileges to the various wines, some without merit and some which have completely disappeared. In his preface to the book *Richesses gastronomiques de France, Les Vins de Bordeaux*, Charles de Lorbac wrote: 'The great vineyards, assuming that they are ably managed and the method of vinification is refined, can in the long run improve the quality of their product. We must admit, however, that apart from human initiative, the main role in the success or failure of a vineyard is played by nature. The small number of good wines is directly linked to the conditions of climate and soil in which the grapes are produced and I think it fruitless to wonder beyond this why Margaux is so exceptional except by a lucky combination of these two factors.'

The present day vineyard of Malescot is divided over five separate areas in Margaux and Soussans, the oldest of which border the Château Margaux property. These are gravelly beds, of similar depth, and generally in the open. The wine is made in the old style, using a vat fermentation process of about 30 days. The wine ages slowly but the bouquet changes from year to year, through a kaleidoscope of scents. The initial raspberry aroma of the new wine matures into blackcurrant, finally to become violet. *Semper ad altum*. Malescot has been fortunate in having Zuger in charge.

Margaux (Château)

♟♟♟♟♟ ♛

1er cru classé

Main area: Margaux, Soussans and Cantenac **Owner:** SCA Château Margaux, 33460 Margaux. Tel (56) 88 70 28. **Director:** Paul Pontallier **Administrator:** Philippe Barre **Chef de culture:** J.-P. Blanchard **Maître de chai:** Jean Grangerou **Surface area of vineyard:** 85 hectares (total property 330 hectares) **Average age of vines:** 30 years **Grape production:** Red: 75% Cabernet-Sauvignon, 20% Merlot, 5% Petit-Verdot and Cabernet-Franc **Production:** 250,000 bottles **Retail sales:** All the main shippers of Bordeaux

---

The high-ranking official of the presidency of the Fifth French Republic (which began in 1958) removed his glasses and raised his eyes towards the flies buzzing around the Louis XV chandelier: 'You must understand, my good man,' he said, 'that to allow the Americans to buy Château Margaux would be like selling them the Eiffel Tower or the Mona Lisa.' I suggested that the Eiffel Tower had little in common with a field of Merlot grapes and that the Mona Lisa was in fact itself an import which could be hung anywhere. He paid no attention to this, however, and continued: 'You must also understand, my good man, that we cannot contradict the express wishes of the President of the Republic in this matter. Margaux must remain French. You are aware, that they have denied permission for Concorde to land in America?' It was thus that the National Distillers Company failed in its bid for the ownership of Château Margaux just as my father and I believed that we had finally found a company with the technical, commercial and financial substance to be to Margaux what Rothschild is to Lafite and Mouton, what Lord Cowdray is to Latour, and what Dillon is to Haut-Brion. For almost two years the proposed sale of Château Margaux was an affair of

The Palladian façade of Château Margaux is well known throughout the world.

state which the press blew up out of all proportion. The two blank lines following represent everything that I have no wish to repeat on this subject: '

Finally, the 'French solution' hoped for by the government was found in the person of André Mentzelopoulos, president of the Félix Potin Company. I would here like to praise the memory of this great man of exceptional qualities, a renowned businessman

of intelligence and taste. The book *Château Margaux* by Nicolas Faith (1981) traces
the history of the property and, if it has several inevitable errors, it is nevertheless a
serious work of reference. Everyone has their own way of telling a story and I should
like to present mine as follows.

In the thirteenth century the property of La Mothe belonged to the Albret family.
Several authors have also stated that it was at one time the property of Edward II, King
of England. From the fifteenth century onwards the affiliation of the barons of La
Mothe-Margaux is well known and includes the names of Montferrand, Durfort,   143

Gimel, Lory, Lestonac, Aulède, Fumel and Hargicourt. For the most part, the estate of La Mothe which, like most of the land around it was part of the Blanquefort property, was passed through the women of the family by marriage alliances. It was at the very beginning of the eighteenth century that the idea of the great wine appeared, brought about by the supremacy of the vineyards of Margaux, Lafite, Latour and Pontac (Haut-Brion) in the courts of Europe and, particularly, with the English aristocracy. The great pioneers of this viticultural revolution were the families of Aulède, Fumel, Ségur and Pontac, who had all established large vineyards and, through their importance, had replaced the practice of naming the wines after the general area, calling them instead after the parish in which they were produced.

The topographical positions of the three best Médoc wines are comparable on every point (one could also include Issan and Beychevelle in this analogy). The châteaux and the outbuildings are built on the eastern edge of pebbly fields, bordered by beds of richer earth. The vineyards are cultivated on the land sloping towards the river, finding variably favourable conditions for growth on the stretches of pebbly soil which form the hillocks. At Château Margaux the stream from Lestonnat, swollen by the brook from Aubion, flows into the western edge of the fishpond. The level of the water-table in the park was improved by this feature, originally dug to provide good drainage for the fields on the gravelly slopes. In the Middle Ages and up to the seventeenth century the channels linking the moats of the château to the river were navigable at high tide. Long narrowboats, known as *aguilas* because of their shape, were seen for centuries on the waterways, preceding the *gabares* common until fifty years ago. They sailed between Margaux and Bordeaux, Bourg, Blaye, Mortagne and Pauillac, ensuring good business links and the transport of the wine barrels: 'Having been loaded at Bordeaux with a large number of barrels and casks, the boats finished their task at Macau, at Bec-d'Ambès, at Margaux and other destinations in the Médoc', wrote Francisque Michel in *Histoire du commerce et de la navigation à Bordeaux* (Bordeaux, 1867). Shipped directly to England, Holland and other destinations, the wines were free of transport surcharge and the toll fees levied in Bordeaux.

The vineyard of La Mothe-Margaux came into being because of the economic opportunities presented by its situation. There all the favours of nature were united to form one of the best wine-growing areas in the world. Competition and co-operation between the families who owned the land added to the success of the wine, and it is thanks to a combination of luck, favourable circumstances and perceptive management that this château is today in a class of its own.

Towards the end of the seventeenth century, Margaux was the property of the Aulède family of Lestonnac. Their steward, by the name of Berlon, used his ingenuity and personal know-how to improve the wine dramatically. Professor René Pijassou rated the vineyard alongside Dom Pérignon because of its numerous innovations in the world of vinification. It was one of the first to separate the white grapes, which till then had traditionally formed up to one-fifth of the production of each vineyard producing red wine. (Only forty years ago, the roots of Sémillon and White Merlot were planted alongside Red Cabernet and Merlot.) In the eighteenth century François d'Aulède died childless, and his sister, Catherine de Fumel, became the owner of Margaux. She continued the cultivation of the property before leaving it to her son Louis, who in turn passed it on to his younger son, Joseph. The latter had an only daughter, Marie-Louise. On the wishes of Louis XV, she married Jean-Baptiste du Barry, the brother-in-law of the infamous countess, the King's mistress. Encumbered by his troublesome surname, Jean-Baptiste du Barry, having tried in vain to appropriate his father-in-law Fumel's coat of arms, instead assumed those of Conti d'Hargicourt, the maiden name of his mother-in-law.

In 1789, several days after the storming of the Bastille, the Count of Hargicourt took himself and his belongings across the Pyrenees. His wife and his ageing father-in-law remained behind to deal with the harsh reality of the Revolution. Margaux was confiscated lock, stock and barrel. A local farmer called Miqueau was enlisted to carry

144

The vats at Château Margaux: noblesse oblige.

out this pillage. It was thus that around 1795, Laure de Fumel, the last of her line, bought back the property with her own money. She went on to marry Count Hector Brane who gave her a son before seeking refuge in Germany. Mme Fumel lost no time in marrying a certain Langsdorff, a man with an import–export business. The oppressive taxation system and a myriad other debts forced Langsdorff to sell the property in favour of a certain marquis of La Colonilla whose real name was, in fact, 145

Bertrand Douat. A lengthy law suit followed and it was seven years before the 'Marquis' was named as lawful owner of the property.

In 1810 Douat de La Colonilla commissioned the architect Emile Combes, a pupil of Victor Louis, to build him a new château. There is nothing remaining to show us what the original building actually looked like, although it probably resembled the country houses of Guyenne. Neither is it known exactly where it was situated, although taking the lay of the land into consideration, it seems likely to have been on the site of the present-day *chais* or in the old park. Six years later the château, the village and the outhouses were finished. After the death of Douat de La Colonilla the property was abandoned for almost twenty years until his three children sold the château to the

GRAND VIN

wealthy banker Aguado, a Castillian by birth. A talented financier, follower of fashion and patron of the arts, Count Aguado, Marquis de Las Marismas, was the leading light of high society in Paris, where his wife was renowned for the brilliance of her salon. The count died in 1842 and his eldest son, Alexander, came into the property, accompanied by his beautiful wife Emily. Alexandre died young and Emily subsequently married her young brother-in-law, Viscount Onoesippe (or Onésime). She later became lady-in-waiting to the Empress Eugénie, who had been her childhood friend, and whom she followed into exile in England. Widowed for the second time, she sold Margaux in 1879 to Count Pillet-Will.

As governor of the Bank of France, Pillet-Will endowed Château Margaux with his personal credit, his name and his coat of arms. Things did not go well, however, for this new owner. His entry into the Médoc vineyard coincided with the economic crisis brought about by the phylloxera epidemic and the outbreak of mildew. Anxious for his reputation and that of his wine, he sold off the harvest in two lots as first- and second-class wine. The term 'grand vin', which now flourishes throughout almost all the varieties in Bordeaux and elsewhere, had no other significance, at the outset, than that of specifying a qualitative selection. In order to outline further the difference between the best and the second-class wines, Pillet-Will introduced a new variety – Le Pavillon Rouge de Château Margaux. It was an offshoot of the Pavillon Blanc, a white wine traditionally produced in small quantities for the personal consumption of the château owners. The Duke of La Trémoille, Pillet-Will's son-in-law, took responsibility for the property on the latter's death in 1911. He sold it ten years later to the Société civile, which my family joined in 1934.

When my father became administrator at Château Margaux there were five unsold harvests in the *chais*, only a third of the vineyard was in any state of production, and the staff had not been paid for six months. He set to work with great care and dedication, uprooting and replanting the most dilapidated fields, tending the exhausted soil and exchanging plots of land with neighbouring producers to restore some kind of unity to the domain. After the war, in 1949, my grandfather Fernand Ginestet and my father succeeded in buying the remaining interests in the Société civile from the Boylandry and Lurton families. My parents courageously decided to move back into the château which had been ransacked by the German troops. My mother undertook the

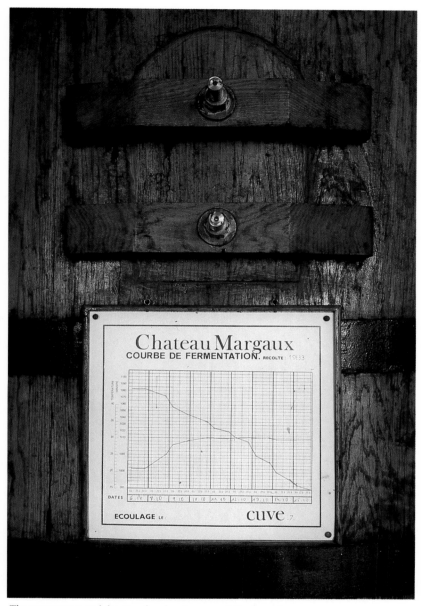

The temperature and density of each vat are carefully charted.

renovation of the interior as well as that of the gardens, and it was she who brought a little warmth back into the rather cold atmosphere of this big house.

On 23 March 1977 a bill of sale was signed by the new Société du Château Margaux (created by André Mentzelopoulos on behalf of the Félix Potin company) and the Ginestet family.

Entering a world of which until then he had known little, André Mentzelopoulos threw himself wholeheartedly into his new role of country gentleman and landowner (his investment was, unfortunately, not profitable in the long term since he died soon 147 after the 1980 harvest). He brought to Margaux a group of first-class specialists, all intent on proving their worth through engineering wide-ranging changes. While the agricultural engineers and oenologists took care of the vineyards and the *chais*, architects, interior decorators, antique dealers and landscape gardeners restored the château and the park. This was obviously a major change of life for Château Margaux. I have my own opinion of this new management, while admiring (from a distance) the power of money. It seems to me that these changes have been made with startling rapidity. The principles of humanity and familiarity, which were part of the driving force behind the Château Margaux of former times, have been replaced with a coldly calculated institutional approach to business. The result should be manifested through the irreproachable quality of the product and indeed I am fully aware of this being the case with the most recently produced vintages. Once more in its long history, Château Margaux has been fortunate in finding an owner worthy of it.

Marquis d'Alesme-Becker (Château) 🍷 🍷 🍷 🍷 🍷

3ᵉ cru classé

Main area: Soussans and Margaux **Owner:** Jean-Claude Zuger, who is responsible for direction, assisted by André Pelletan, *maître de chai* **Surface area of vineyard:** 8.64 hectares (total property 31.5 hectares) **Average age of vines:** 25 years **Grape production:** Cabernets, Merlots and Verdots **Production:** 50,000 bottles **Local sales:** Tel (56) 88 70 27, **and by mail order** (France only): Château Marquis d'Alesme, 33460 Margaux **Retail sales:** Abroad, shipped direct

Marquis d'Alesme-Becker is a phantom variety which has haunted the Margaux appellation for more than a century, occasionally rattling its *3ᵉ cru classé* chains which have saved it from complete oblivion. Had the Marquis d'Alesme been a bourgeois *cru*, we should not have paid it such great attention.

Once upon a time, in the charming village of Margaux, there lived a friendly Marquis called d'Alesme. The gods smiled on his property, and his small but well-tended vineyard produced fine ripe grapes with which he made exquisite wine. All this happened a long time ago, at the start of the twelfth century A.D. Two centuries later, a connoisseur named Becker (or Bekker) discovered this little orphaned patch of land by chance, while walking through the vineyards of the lords of Margaux, and immediately decided to adopt it. The child was acknowledged by true connoisseurs and christened Marquis d'Alesme-Becker. Without even growing, it wormed its way to the head of the *3ᵉ cru classé* in the 1855 classification. This passed without comment, but

The Château Desmirail, now the Château Marquis d'Alesme-Becker.

its new father, Sznajderski, was extremely proud. The villainous Arthur de Gassowski took advantage of Sznajderski's age to buy the property from him. He resold it at the end of the century to the good M. Chaix d'Est-Ange, who shared his attention between it and Château Lascombes. The English, seeking revenge for the Hundred Years War, had meanwhile managed to raise the Union Jack at Malescot Saint-Exupéry and they bought the Marquis d'Alesme-Becker from Chaix d'Est-Ange's son. Finding the name rather hard to pronounce, Messieurs W. H. Chaplin & Co. Ltd, employing a logic of which they alone held the secret, renamed the vintage Malescot. They even transformed this name into 'Male Scot' to give it a bit of local Scottish colour. The ladies of London society were enraptured: 'Please give me a kilt of Male Scot' they cried.

In 1938 the mining engineer Zuger, sensing the insecurity of his Alsatian property, returned to Margaux and bought the Château Desmirail. Both Desmirail and Marquis d'Alesme had vanished as far as wine production was concerned. It was then that the Good Fairy appeared and said: 'I declare that the Marquis d'Alesme-Becker should have a new home and that this home should be Desmirail. I declare that Desmirail should produce wine once more and that should be the wine of Lucien Lurton.' All this was achieved in the twinkling of an eye. In 1969, the situation was so complicated that Féret, in the twelfth amended edition of *Bordeau et ses vins*, printed on one page a photograph of a fine Louis XIII château captioned 'Château Marquis d'Alesme-Becker, 3ᵉ cru classé'. On the following page was an ancient engraving of the same château captioned 'Château Desmirail, 3ᵉ cru classé'. All this had not halted the printing of an anniversary label, in 1966, for the 350th anniversary of the variety.

The variety of Marquis d'Alesme-Becker is now in the capable hands of Jean-Claude Zuger, son of Paul and brother of Roger Zuger (see Malescot Saint-Exupéry). He restocked the vineyard in 1977 and, in 1979, withdrew from the family business and constructed his own *chais*. Since then, he has proudly used the noble label headed by the coronet of the Marquis d'Alesme. One might hope that the horseshoe printed beneath will indeed prove lucky for him. The variety is only a step away from being

The programme for extending the buildings is still in progress at Marquis de Terme.

'Marquis d'Alesme-Zuger.' And, indeed, why not? One has seen many other even stranger changes in the Médoc. Jean-Claude Zuger is a local and makes good wine which has the privilege of being a *3ᵉ cru classé*.

Marquis de Terme (Château)

Main area: Margaux **Owners:** Pierre-Louis, Philippe and Jean Sénéclauze **Steward:** Jean-Pierre Hugon **Chef de culture:** Pierre Salignan **Maître de chai:** Alain Gouinaud **Surface area of vineyard:** 35 hectares (total property 85 hectares) **Average age of vines:** 25 years **Grape production:** 35% Cabernet-Sauvignon, 35% Merlot, 15% Cabernet-Franc, 5% Petit-Verdot **Production:** 150,000 bottles **Local sales:** Tel (56) 88 30 01 **Retail sales:** Société des Vins Sénéclauze, 164 boulevard de Plombières, 13307 Marseille Cedex

4ᵉ cru classé

Between the seventeenth and eighteenth centuries, Margaux and the surrounding area was home for a wide section of the French aristocracy, from equerries to grand dukes. Many of the present-day varieties of wine remind us of these bygone days. The fearless, shameless Lord Peguichan was one of the youngest sons of the house of Gascogne. Through his mother's family he was also Marquis de Terme, probably descended from the Terme family of Armagnac. He courted Mlle Ledoulx, the niece of the Lord of Rauzan, and on 16 December 1762 he married her. That the date should be so precisely recorded is extremely interesting, since not much more is known; at the end of the eighteenth century there is no trace of this son of Gascogne. Several authors have written that the vineyard was created by uniting several small varieties scattered throughout Cantenac, Margaux, Arsac and Soussans. Their names, no longer current, are Léoville-Cantenac, L'Isle, Sibille and Phénix. Until now I have been unable to establish the authentic origin but it is also rumoured that the Marquis de Terme wines were once MacDaniel.

What is certain is that Oscar Sollberg, a rich merchant, restored the wine's reputation in the middle of the nineteenth century. Between 1830 and 1840 he completely rebuilt the vineyard, and it was thanks to him that in 1855 it was classified as a *4ᵉ cru*. At that time, Sollberg was one of the most important men in the Margaux commune. He had many confrontations with the local authorities because of his intention of producing wine using rich beds of earth. Long before Margaux had its own appellation, a certain confusion reigned between the Marquis de Terme wines produced on gravelly soil, and those from the richer earth; the latter are nowadays sold quite distinctly under the label of Domaine des Gondats. As for the main variety, it is clearly obvious that the old spelling of Thermes has been simplified to Terme.

In his *Encyclopédie des vins* Alexis Lichine observes that the Marquis de Terme vineyards are cultivated in an impeccable fashion, while the vinification sometimes leaves a lot to be desired. The veracity of the first half of this statement is obvious, even to a casual stroller in Margaux village, where several of the Terme vineyards lie alongside the town buildings. As to the vinification, Marquis de Terme has managed to achieve an extremely high level of produce per hectare, several times beating the previous record set through Margaux. This is obviously not the best way to improve on quality. Château Marquis de Terme used to be notoriously under-equipped as far as *chais*, vat houses and other production buildings were concerned, but over the last few years the new owners, the Sénéclauze family, have implemented a wide-ranging improvement plan. The new *chais* are large, modern and well designed. There is also a reception room for visitors and the vat house and other outbuildings are now worthy of a *cru classé*. Further constructive changes are envisaged.

The Marquis de Terme wine is characteristically strong and robust. It is generally rather tannic and, as a result, not at its best when young. The high proportion of Petit-Verdot grapes once accentuated its natural acidity but, today, the wine seems more balanced and, curiously enough, it is in the most difficult years that Marquis de Terme produces its best wines in comparison with the surrounding vineyards. Nevertheless it has a distinct local accent which, though it may never equal the great delicacy and smoothness of the best Margaux wines, clearly reminds us that its former owner, de Peguichan, was a Gascogne pure and simple.

Marsac Séguineau (Château)

Main area: Soussans **Owner:** S C du Château Marsac Séguineau, Tel (56) 88 30 41 **Director:** Patrice Baudieras, who oversees both direction and production, assisted by the oenologist Bernard Monteau **Surface area of vineyard:** 8 hectares (total property 11 hectares) **Average age of vines:** 15 years **Grape production:** $\frac{2}{3}$ Cabernet-Sauvignon, $\frac{1}{3}$ Merlot **Production:** 35,000 bottles **Sold exclusively by:** Mestrezat SA, 17 cours de la Martinique, BP 90, 33027 Bordeaux Cedex, Tel (56) 52 11 46

cru bourgeois

The coronet which decorates the classically simple label of this wine belongs to the Count of Robieu who, in 1866, merged the *cru bourgeois* of Séguineau-Deyries with other plots of land in the Marsac area. He refused to give his own name to the variety, believing that Marsac Séguineau sounded much better. At the beginning of the century, the property was owned by Mme Vast, who enlarged the vineyard by purchasing new tracts of land, probably from either Lascombes or Malescot. The property changed hands several times soon after, belonging to Marcelin, Villenfranca and Pécresse, who sold all his vineyard property at Soussans, Avensan, Moulis and Listrac to a company combining the best wines of the area under the guidance of Lucien Lurton and the company of Mestrezat-Preller de Bordeaux (nowadays Mestrezat SA). When this company dissolved, Marsac Séguineau was put under the control of Mestrezat.

The property is made up of two vineyards which are both situated near Marsac. The soil is clay-like and gravelly. The wine is produced by modern methods, which help to diminish the tannin content for a smoother effect. A publicity brochure recommends that it should be served at between 14 and 16 degrees centigrade. I myself am not in favour of wines served too warm, but would suggest that 18 to 20 degrees would be a better temperature, as with all Margaux wines.

Martinens (Château)

cru bourgeois supérieur

Main area: Cantenac **Owners:** Simone Dulos and Jean-Pierre Seynat-Dulos **Director:** Jean-Pierre Seynat-Dulos (director of La Société fermière) and Mme Dulos (director of La Société civile) **Steward** M. Delille **Maître de chai:** Delille father and son **Surface area of vineyard:** 30 hectares (total property 60 hectares) **Average age of vines:** 23 and 13 years **Grape production:** Red: 40% Merlot, 30% Cabernet-Sauvignon, 20% Petit-Verdot, 10% Cabernet-Franc **Production:** 85,000 bottles **Local sales:** Tel (56) 88 71 37, **and by mail order:** Château Martinens, Cantenac, 33460 Margaux **Retail sales:** Maison Audy, Cavif, Cordier, Ets Vinicoles de Gironde, Germe, Janoueix, Ets Lebegue, Moueix, Pierre Jean, André Quancard, Quien, Vedrenne

Situated on the western edge of the Cantenac commune and to the south-west of Margaux lies the elegant Château Martinens. Beside the small surrounding park stand the *chais* and the vat houses, all built in a similar functional style. There is always a warm welcome at Martinens, and Mme Simone Dulos and her son, Jean-Pierre Seynat-Dulos, are extremely hospitable to all visitors. This warmth extends to the *maître de chai* Delille and his son who, when the owners are away, make sure that every visitor feels at home as soon as he enters their storehouse.

The property was owned in the eighteenth century by three British sisters, Ann, Jane and Mary White, who used Martinens as a holiday home. In 1776 they sold the property to Pierre Changeur, a businessman in Bordeaux. He extended the property and started building the present château, but finally sold it without completing his plan of modernization. His successor, Louis Mascou from Guadeloupe, in turn sold the property to the Count de Beauregard, alias François-Auguste de Sautter. He was consul-general of Tuscany and chamberlain of the French Empire. He came to Médoc hoping to relieve his boredom with the white wines of Vaux, produced on the family property of Beauregard. When he died his two daughters, Clémentine and Gertrude, sold Martinens to Jules Jadouin who was well known throughout Margaux at the end of the nineteenth century (see Angludet). His son-in-law, Jacques Lebègue, was in

153

One is always sure of a warm welcome at Martinens.

charge of running the property until 1936, and was also the first magistrate in the Cantenac commune. For the following nine years, Martinens became Swiss property once more, before being bought by the Dulos-Seynat family. Jean-Pierre Seynat, originally from the south-west of France, is the present mayor of Cantenac. He has now become the complete gentleman farmer, producing in the most elegant manner wine that is widely appreciated.

Maucaillou (Domaine de)

cru artisan

Main area: Soussans **Owner:** Georges Rabi, who oversees both direction and production, Tel (56) 88 36 89 **Surface area of vineyard:** 2.5 hectares (total property 18 hectares) **Average age of vines:** 20–25 years **Grape production:** Traditional **Production:** A dozen or so *tonneaux*, usually sold to various shippers **Retail sales:** D'Arfeuille, in Libourne

The plateau of Maucaillou is found on the extreme north-east of Margaux, near Château Paveil. Georges Rabi himself works the family property, which includes a small vineyard. Well sited on beds of gravelly soil, the vineyard is remarkable in that it measures exactly eight Bordeaux '*journaux*'. The surface area of a '*journal*' (also known as *journau* or *journée*) was equivalent to the area a wine-grower could work in one day. According to the type of soil in the different wine-growing regions and the slope of the land, the exact area of a *journal* varied widely. An average measurement was established for the more gravelly areas which measured a *journal* as $\frac{1}{3}$ of a hectare. The owners who employed a contractor to work their vineyards did so on the basis of an agreed price. Each area of vines contracted in this way was calculated as eight *journaux*, being approximately 2.5 hectares. Georges Rabi is living evidence of this former practice and employs himself to cultivate his 8 *journaux* of Cabernet, Malbec and Verdot. He would be well advised to begin bottling his produce on site.

Monbrison (Château)

cru bourgeois

Main area: Arsac **Owners:** Elizabeth Davis and Sons **Director:** Mme E. Davis, assisted by her son Jean-Luc Vonderheyden **Surface area of vineyard:** 14 hectares (total property 25 hectares) **Average age of vines:** 20 years **Grape production:** 35% Merlot, 30% Cabernet-Sauvignon, 30% Cabernet-Franc, 5% Verdot **Production:** 65,000 bottles **Local sales:** Tel (56) 88 34 52, **and by mail order** (France only): Château Monbrison, Arsac, 33460 Margaux **Retail sales:** Sold directly to foreign importers

The family atmosphere of the delightful Monbrison.

One fine summer morning some years ago, the chief adjutant of the Macau gendarme brigade arrived with great ceremony at Monbrison in Arsac. He knew the house well, having visited it several times, usually just to say hello. This time, however, his official bearing warned Mme Davis that something was wrong. 'Can I help, adjutant?' 'Well, Madame, I would like to know if you remember what happened on the eighteenth of July.' 'Well, sir, I really can't think. As far as I remember, nothing out of the ordinary.' 'Do you remember the storm?' 'Let me think, yes ... I think I do.' 'And that it threatened to hail?' 'Ah yes, yes, now I'm with you; there's certainly no rest at harvest time!' 'Madame, did you fire any anti-hail rockets?' 'Well of course! I'm always the first to know when there's a hail storm on the way.' 'At what time was that approximately?' 'Let me think ... It was definitely before lunch, it must have been about twelve or half past.' 'And do you remember having heard an aeroplane overhead at that time?' 'Well, they pass by quite often; we are on the flight path for Bordeaux-Mérignac ... Yes I suppose it's possible. Why?' 'Well, Madame, you hit it.' A mail plane had taken off from Mérignac and maintained a low altitude under the storm, looking for a clear spell to climb. Mme Davis, having seen the great copper-coloured clouds from a distance (it is this colour which distinguishes them as carrying hailstones) had fired her anti-hail rocket of silver iodine, which exploded at some 400 metres, damaging the aircraft's steering system. The pilot, frightened rather than injured, was forced to turn round and land for repair.

Mme Davis is half American on her father's side. He was Robert Meacham-Davis, commissioner of the Red Cross in the Balkans during the First World War. He bought Monbrison in 1921. Betty Davis and her three sons, Bruno, Jean-Luc and Laurent, are of that fair-skinned complexion which makes one think of the pioneers in Texas and Oregon two centuries ago. This impression is heightened by the sight of the three brothers climbing the highest pine trees around the château, with their rifles in their hands. Pigeons and thrushes do not live long at Monbrison as Bruno, Jean-Luc and Laurent Vonderheyden are the best shots in the area.

Monbrison is a charmingly romantic house, part of which dates from the seventeenth century. The property owes its name to the Conquéré de Monbrison family which owned it for more than a hundred years. The vineyard is planted around the château on a fine, flat, gravelly area. It was entirely replanted, some twenty years ago, after the frosts of 1956. It is now Jean-Luc Vonderheyden who is in charge of the grape-growing and wine-making. He is joint mayor of Arsac and president of the commune's wine producers' association. Monbrison produces wines almost as robust as its owners. They are always deep in colour and need several years to develop a bouquet and finesse.

Moncabon (Enclos de) ⚱ → Rauzan-Gassies

Mongravey (Château)

cru artisan

Main area: Arsac **Owner:** Régis Bernarleau, who oversees both direction and production, Tel (56) 88 74 45 **Surface area of vineyard:** 4.3 hectares (total property 6 hectares) **Average age of vines:** 18 for approximately 1.8 hectares; the rest are much older **Grape production:** 54% Cabernet-Sauvignon, 37% Merlot, 9% Cabernet-Franc **Production:** 15,000 bottles **Sold locally and by mail order. Retail sales:** Very few, since the majority is sold locally

Château Mongravey is a new variety created by the regrouping of a number of plots of land in Arsac. Like his father before him, Régis Bernaleau has taken great care of the family property, some of which is planted with very old vinestock. During the last eighteen years, however, a small amount of replanting has taken place. In three or four years' time, production will be up to about 25,000 bottles. These will be sold locally as at present, and also through the Bordeaux shippers. A neighbour of Château Monbrison, Mongravey is also close to it in quality.

Montbrun (Château)

cru bourgeois

Main area: Cantenac **Owner:** J. Lebègue et Cie SA, Saint-Emilion, Tel (56) 51 31 05 **Directors:** Jacques and Alain de Coninck **Chef de culture:** M. Munes **Surface area of vineyard:** 8 hectares (total property 12 hectares) **Average age of vines:** 20 years **Grape production:** 75% Merlot, 25% Cabernet **Production:** 40,000 bottles **Retail sales:** J. Lebègue et Cie SA, 33330 Saint-Emilion

From the moment they bought Palmer (see below), the Péreire family were unable to restore it to its former glory under the celebrated general. Several pieces of the puzzle were missing, lost by the former owner during his financial difficulties. The Jadouin family were at that time important land-owners in the Cantenac area. It was, in fact, Jules Jadouin who first introduced Montbrun wines. The vineyard was set up as a completely separate enterprise from the larger Palmer business and, at the end of the last century, Jadouin's son-in-law, Jacques Lebègue, built a large house designed by M. Minvielle, 'one of the most distinguished architects in the Bordeaux area'. Château Montbrun was finally classified as a *cru bourgeois supérieur*. (The most recent editions of Féret's *Bordeaux et ses vins* still draw attention to the château even though it was completely destroyed by fire in 1956.) After the Palmer property, Montbrun is the second largest vineyard in the village of Issan. It has long been used as a *chai de commerce* for Maison J. Lebègue et Cie. The present directors, Jacques and Alain de Coninck, have diverted this business to Saint-Emilion, and the Montbrun production buildings have been restored to their original use.

The Montbrun property now includes several plots of land all centred around the old Palmer estate. Montbrun produces smooth rich wines because of the abundance of Merlot grapes in its manufacture. These wines are extremely popular throughout northern France and Europe where they are widely available. Château Montbrun is every inch the equal of the Pontac-Lynch and Vincent vineyards, in the same area of Issan, and a worthy holder of the *cru bourgeois de Margaux*.

Notton (Ch.) 🏚 → Brane-Cantenac

Palmer (Château)

3ᵉ cru classé

Main area: Cantenac **Owner:** SCI Château Palmer **Director:** B. Bouteiller **Chef de culture:** Claude Chardon **Maître de chai:** Yves Chardon **Surface area of vineyard:** 45 hectares (total property 52 hectares) **Average age of vines:** 35 years **Grape production:** 55% Cabernet-Sauvignon, 39% Merlot, 6% Cabernet-Franc **Production:** 150,000 bottles **Exclusive retail sales:** Société Sichel, 19 quai de Bacalan, 33000 Bordeaux; Société Mähler-Besse, 49 rue Camille-Godard, 33000 Bordeaux

Ten years ago Professor Pijassou, a student of Henri Enjalbert and tireless historian of the Médoc vineyards, wrote a long article on Château Palmer in the *Revue historique de Bordeaux et du département de la Gironde*. Reading this impressive work of reference gives one a startling insight into the working conditions of the eighteenth century winegrowers and of the great families of the Médoc. The wine-growing commune of Cantenac towards the end of the Ancien Régime is also covered, as are the house of Foix de Candale and the history of Issan and the domain of Angludet. There is also some interesting information on the amount of trade conducted by ship which, in my opinion, has always been largely underestimated in the history of the development of the Médoc vineyards.

The history of Château Palmer, however, prior to the nineteenth century, remains open to doubt. I can in no way claim to be better qualified than René Pijassou to describe the early history of this noble house, and so will leave it to him to do so.

It would appear that a piece of the domain of Issan passed into the hands of the Gascq family, who were councillors in the Bordeaux Parliament. At the end of the eighteenth century. Mme Marie Burnet de La Ferriere, widow of M. Blaise-Jean-

Charles-Alexander de Gascq, was indisputably the sole owner of the property, which comprised vineyards of some 50 hectares in area located in Cantenac and Margaux. The wine produced was well known at Versailles under the name of Château de Gascq.

At this point, Professor Pijassou refers to Féret's 1874 edition of the *Statistique générale de la Gironde*. As for the Versailles connection, and Richelieu's passion for Gascq wines, that could well be yet another of the legends of our fine country. M. Pijassou, nevertheless, is quite right in thinking that Issan had already been divided fifty years before the Revolution. It would seem inevitable that such an extensive property should be divided among the members of the owning family. One can trace the movements of the Gascq family in the social, economic and political life of Bordeaux and, by all appearances, they had little choice but to follow the fashion and have their own Médoc vineyard. (The Gascq – or Gasques – family were probably originally from the modern-day Tarn-et-Garonne.) It is well known that a vineyard cut off from its original name is like a body without the head, and all this leads us to surmise that the Gascqs gave their name to properties once attached to Château d'Issan. In any case, in 1855 both Issan and Palmer were classified as *3ᵉ crus*, which justly reflects their original association.

After Gascq's death, his widow managed to get through the Reign of Terror without losing the property. In 1814, she sold the Château de Gascq to Major Charles Palmer, general officer and member of Wellington's army. He probably came back to Bordeaux on his return from the Spanish campaign after the defeat of Napoleon at Vittoria. Paris was surrounded on 11 April 1814, and Issan was purchased on 16 June. Over the next twenty years Palmer enlarged his property in every direction. He bought everything that he could, beginning with a large part of Dubignon-Talbot (see Larruau). Not satisfied with this he went on to purchase Montbrun, Boston and other lands at Issan. But in 1834 his wife decided to cut loose and took out a mortgage on his property. From then on, there was a slow but inexorable decline. The château was confiscated in 1844 and run by the mortgage office for ten years. It was finally bought by the Péreires, a family of Portuguese Jews with a talent for finding the best financial investments. (Arcachon was another of their projects).

Isaac Rodrigue-Péreire, a great rival of the Rothschild family, bought Palmer just before the classification of 1855. It was by then too late for them to have much effect on the wine classification, but the family wasted no time in restoring the vineyard and constructing a new château on a piece of land formerly owned by Issan. It is frequently said that Palmer should have a higher classification. I would dare to suggest that if Palmer, Issan and the other lands of the former houses of Foix de Candale and Castelnau d'Essenault had been preserved as one piece, they would have been jointly awarded the title of *premier cru classé*. We should not forget that the quality of the Médoc wines is largely due to the size and variety of the lands. In 1938 Palmer was again divided and taken over by a Société civile, which remains in control to this day

The neo-renaissance Château Palmer is a great tourist attraction in the Médoc.

under the direction of the Mähler and the Sichels. In 1957 the Palmer property was enlarged by the purchase of the Desmirail vineyard.

It is only fitting that I should mention the 'trois Chardons' of Palmer, Pierre and his two sons, Claude and Yves, the real producers of this work of art. The Palmer wines have been tremendously successful, and balance body and delicacy in the true Margaux style. For the final word on this variety, let us consider the words of Nicholas Faith on Château Margaux: 'Its southern neighbour, Château Palmer, whose sunny slopes run alongside the best land of Margaux, is the only vineyard in the commune which, in certain years, can truly be comparable in quality.' This is, to me, a statement of indisputable fact.

Paveil de Luze (Château)

Main area: Soussans **Owner:** GFA du Château Paveil, Tel (56) 88 30 03 **Director:** Geoffroy de Luze, assisted by René Fort **Surface area of vineyard:** 24 hectares (total property 120 hectares) **Average age of vines:** 15 years **Grape production:** Red: 70% Cabernet, 30% Merlot **Production:** 120,000 bottles **Retail sales:** Groupement Français des Vins (GFV), Bordeaux

cru bourgeois

With 15 hectares of parkland, game reserve and gardens, a seventeenth-century *château-chai* and 24 hectares of vineyards spreading out from the entrance like a green and white fan, Château Paveil is a wine-grower's dream. In this model vineyard can be seen all the signs of true good management and taste. Part of the old house is still occupied and beside it stand the *chai*, the vat houses and the farm; behind them is a small village and, further still, between the château and the edge of the forest, is a pool where one can fish for tench, carp and pike. During harvest time anyone walking early in the woods will find the cèpes and chanterelles growing there.

The Luze family have lived at Paveil for more than a century. This noble family, originally from Neuchâtel, emigrated to the United States over a hundred years ago. The two young men, Alfred and Louis-Philippe, threw themselves enthusiastically into the commercial life of the New World, becoming importers of specialist foods. Naturally enough, wine was one of the most sought-after products. Some time later, Alfred returned to Europe to establish better supplies and shippers. Finding that Bordeaux offered everything he required, he settled there, and in 1862 he bought Le Paveil from

At Paveil, one roof houses both the family and the wine.

a businessman, M. Minvielle. The property had originally, during the reign of Louis XIII, been owned by the Chevalier de Bretonneau, who received the lands as a dowry for his wife, yet another member of the Rauzan family. The strange thing about the buildings is that both the living quarters and wine-producing areas are housed under one roof. This is a great advantage if one is thirsty during the night, as one can sample a drop of the new wine without leaving the house.

The wine produced at Paveil is as distinguished as its owner. It is inclined more to delicacy than to fullness, and its slight bitterness when young quickly changes into a much finer bouquet. It ages well, remaining extremely smooth. The vineyards are planted on three flat pebbly beds and, enjoying some of the warmest sunshine in Margaux, they produce some of the highest yields in the region. The owners of Château Paveil de Luze are brought together in the GFA (Groupement Français Agricole). These include the Baron Geoffroy de Luze and his three children: Mme Denis Blanchard-Dignac, M. Frédéric de Luze and Mlle Catherine de Luze.

Situated on the extreme west to the north of Margaux, Château Paveil de Luze has been a faithful sentinel for almost four centuries

Pavillon Blanc du Château Margaux

Main area: Soussans **Owner:** SCA Château Margaux, 33460 Margaux **Surface area of vineyard:** 11 hectares **Grape production:** 100% White Sauvignon **Production:** 40,000 bottles **Retail sales:** Seeing this white wine listed as a Margaux *cru* is about as likely as seeing a white blackbird

This wine is certainly more of a curiosity than a work of art. It is really pure vanity for an area so well known for its red wine to produce white. As a kind of souvenir of the old Margaux, there have always been vines producing white grapes at Château Margaux. They were originally planted at the far end of the property, on the areas known as le Désert and la Fontanelle. In these areas there is a predominance of chalky soil near the surface, which is extremely rare in the Haut-Médoc. At the beginning of the century, a small vineyard flourished there, composed of white Sauvignons, Sémillons and a few Muscadelles. I can also remember a strip of white Merlots (a variety now out of favour) which grew at the edge of the old kitchen garden till the end of the last war. This combination produced an unpretentious white wine for domestic use.

Pierre Ginestet increased this modest production by planting Sauvignon vines at the edge of the Margaux appelation area, near the start of the richer soils and on the excellent pebbly plateau of Virefougasse at Soussans. This latter site, however, has an unfortunate tendency to freeze in spring, and the present owners of Château Margaux have made great progress in protecting it against the cold.

The only *appellation contrôlée* possible for this variety would be '*Bordeaux supérieur*', as there is no familiar appellation for white wine in the Médoc. What was once a small family project has now become a substantial source of production. The selling price of Pavillon Blanc du Château Margaux has also drastically increased, almost in direct proportion.

Pavillon Rouge du Château Margaux
→ Margaux

Pichecan (Château de)

cru artisan

Main area: Soussans **Owner:** Jean-Marc Boutain, who oversees both direction and production **Surface area of vineyard:** 1.7 hectares (total property 3.5 hectares) **Average age of vines:** 12 years **Grape production:** 60% Cabernet-Sauvignon, 30% Merlot, 10% Petit-Verdot **Production:** 6000 bottles **Local sales:** Tel (56) 88 73 04, **and by mail order** (in France and abroad): Château de Pichecan, Le Grand-Soussans, 33460 Margaux

In the older editions of Féret's *Bordeaux et ses vins*, from 1886 onwards, mention is made of Château Grand-Soussans. This variety has now completely disappeared, following a series of bad harvests. Jean-Marc Boutain lives at Le Grand-Soussans surrounded by his 3 hectare empire, half of which is covered by the vineyard. The whole forms the kingdom of Pichecan, a name that might conjure up ideas of medieval Rome but which, in fact, is nothing as poetic in the local dialect.

One must get up very early in the morning and be well liked, if one wants to sample the Pichecan product. Jean-Marc Boutain, chief justice of Pichecan, is very selective about the clients he chooses for his wine.

Pontac-Lynch (Château)

cru bourgeois supérieur

Main area: Margaux **Owner:** GFA du Château Pontac-Lynch **Director:** S. Bondon, who oversees both direction and production **Surface area of vineyard:** 9 hectares (total property 26 hectares) **Average age of vines:** 20 years **Grape production:** 100% red **Production:** 35,000–40,000 bottles **Local sales:** Tel (56) 88 30 04, **and by mail order** (in France and abroad): Château Pontac-Lynch, 33460 Margaux **Retail sales:** Groupement des Vignerons du Bordelais, 33460 Margaux; SA du Vivier, Immeuble Concorde, 22 quai de Bacalan, 33300 Bordeaux

What a strange combination these two names are! They bring together two ideal varieties containing the very essence of the great wines of the eighteenth and nineteenth centuries. Over a very small area, covering perhaps some 500–700 metres, one can trace a semi-circle of different *crus* surrounding Château Margaux. Clockwise these are: Issan, Monbrun, Vincent, Palmer, Rausan-Ségla, Rauzan-Gassies (and Marquis de Terme a little further off), Durfort-Vivens, Malescot Saint-Exupéry, Larruau,

An avenue of palm trees leads to the Pontac-Lynch vineyard.

Desmirail-Marquis d'Alesme-Becker and La Gurgue. I mention here only the châteaux themselves, not necessarily their vineyards which tend to be scattered throughout the whole appellation area. But in this abundance, what has happened to Pontac-Lynch? It falls squarely at the centre of this well-ordered arrangement. It is hidden away at the end of an avenue of palm trees, brought back to the Médoc at the start of the century by some braggart after the conquest of Algeria. It is certainly small, but nonetheless significant, straddling the edge of the gravelly soil and the beginning of the richer earth, like its close neighbours Château Issan to the left and Château Margaux to the right. One can imagine what Sempé would make of this idea: a small house with three bicycles in front, jammed between two big mansions with the latest model limousines outside.

Pontac-Lynch has long suffered from its impressive neighbours for two reasons. First because of its size (one tenth that of Château Margaux); secondly, because the vineyards are a little low-lying (but the drainage is perfect and the stronger soil encourages the vines).

Owner, general director, steward, *chef de culture* and *maître de chai*: Serge Bondon. Business agent: the former. He is also a crack shot. There is certainly no good reason why M. Bondon should not produce excellent wines. Besides this, between 1741 and 1774, Pontac-Lynch sold all its meagre production at much higher prices than the *grands crus* classified in 1855 – another excellent reason for celebrating the worth of this vineyard. The variety has recently received gold medals for its perseverance and is shaping up well to the responsibility of bearing the names of Pontac-Lynch.

Pontet-Chappaz *(Château)*

Main area: Arsac **Owner:** Vignobles Rocher Cap-de-Rive, 33330 Saint-Etienne-de-Lisse, Tel (57) 40 08 28 **Director:** M. Lafaye, Tel (57) 40 18 28 **Steward:** M. Caussan in Ordonnac, Tel (56) 41 11 67 **Surface area of vineyard:** 7 hectares **Average age of vines:** Approximately 15 years **Grape production:** Cabernets, Merlots and Verdots **Production:** Unknown **Marketing:** address as above

Château Pontet-Chappaz at Arsac is one of a group of vineyards belonging to a Belgian, M. Geens. This 7 hectare property stretches unbroken over the gravelly terrace beside Monbrison. There is no 'château' on its label, as there is not a single building on the property. Some of the grapes are produced and harvested at Arsac and are then transported to Saint-Germain-d'Esteuil, near Lesparre, where they are crushed, fermented and bottled under the name of the Société des Vignobles Rocher-Cap-de-Rive, at Saint-Magne-de-Castillon, near Castillon-la-Bataille. The *chef de culture* is M. Caussan, who lives not far from Plautignan in Ordonnac, the southern suburb of Potensac in Médoc. The director is M. Lafaye at Saint-Etienne-de-Lisse to the north of Saint-Emilion.

The name of Pontet-Chappaz unites two families who spent the worst part of the Revolution in Margaux. It is plain to see how the history of France is printed on the labels of its wine.

Pouget *(Château)*

4e cru classé

Main area: Cantenac **Owner:** GFA des Châteaux Boyd-Cantenac et Pouget **Director:** Pierre Guillemet, who has responsibility for production and wine-making under M. Emile Peynaud **Surface area of vineyard:** 10 hectares (total property 60 hectares) **Average age of vines:** 40 years **Grape production:** Red: 56% Cabernet-Sauvignon, 30% Merlot, 4% Cabernet-Franc **Production:** 47,000 bottles **Local sales:** Tel (56) 88 30 58, **and by mail order** (France only): Château Pouget, Cantenac, 33460 Margaux **Retail sales:** MM. Dubos Frères et Cie, 24 quai des Chartrons, 33000 Bordeaux

This property once belonged to the canon of Saint-Emilion, chaplain of the largest body of worshippers in Bordeaux. This priest was extremely rich thanks to his grateful flock who, amazed by his rhetoric, gladly donated the money required by a man so interested in quality wine. He was called Etienne Monteil and his successful career spanned the second half of the seventeenth century. A hundred years later this sacred earth reverted to the ownership of François-Antoine Pouget, sole legatee of the Monteil-Dorchiac-Ducasse family. He was not one to turn his nose up at this gift from the gods, and good Bordeaux citizen that he was, he bestowed his name on the property. He had one daughter, Claire, who married the lawyer Pierre François de Chavaille. This young man was also the secretary-general of Bordeaux town.

By the nineteenth century, however, Pouget, like many other varieties, had been transformed through sales and partitions of its land. Before the 1855 classification, it was most often a *3ᵉ cru*. By the time of the official classification, however, it was no longer at the peak of its career and was finally placed among the *4ᵉ crus*.

The Elie-Guillemet family purchased the château in 1906. M. P. Elie was lucky enough to buy two hectares from the Rauzan-Gassies vineyard, on the southern side of Cantenac. Pierre Guillemet, who also owns Château Boyd-Cantenac, is an excellent wine-grower.

The Chavaille coat of arms is still printed on the label; at one time this was accompanied by a motto which described the position of the silver heart on a red background, a cock on a blue background and a lion on black. I find the lyricism of the last line irresistible:

> *L'amour dessus ton coeur étendra sa puissance,*
> *Ton verbe sera clair comme le chant du coq,*
> *A l'égal du lion tu ne craindras le choc,*
> *Si de cestuy nectar tu te remplis la panse.*

In my opinion we need another two lines to perfect the poem:

> *Le parfum, la bonté, le charme et l'élégance,*
> *Font du Château Pouget un délicieux Médoc.*

Prieuré-Lichine (Château)

4ᵉ cru classé

Main area: Cantenac **Owner:** SA Château Prieuré-Lichine **Chef de culture:** Albert Birades **Maître de chai:** Armand Labarère **Surface area of vineyard:** 60 hectares (total property 60 hectares) **Grape production:** Red: 52% Cabernet-Sauvignon, 33% Merlot, 8% Petit-Verdot, 7% Cabernet-Franc **Production:** 300,000 bottles **Local sales:** Tel (56) 88 36 28, **and by mail order:** Château Prieuré-Lichine, Cantenac, 33460 Margaux **Retail sales:** All the major Bordeaux shippers

The Cantenac priory (*prieuré*) was a Benedictine monastery, so old that according to legend it even pre-dates St Benedict, founder of the Order. Their vineyard ensured the congregation a steady income, like the Carthusians' Green Chartreuse and the Carmelites' Eau de Cologne. This sacred land was hallowed by the local gentry who showed their piety in loaning the monks three labourers to tend the vines, two mules to transport the supporting stakes and a pair of oxen to prepare the ground, while the peasants dug out the '*cavaillon*' as a kind of purgatory among the Cabernets. (*Cavaillon* is a Médoc term for the amount of land remaining between two vine stalks after they have been exposed. The *cavaillons* are dug with a pick, the earth being placed in the central furrow.)

The present prior of Château Prieuré is Alexis Lichine, after whom the wine is now named Château Prieuré-Lichine. There is little written evidence of the activities of the previous priors, but this latter is well known for his ever-open vault. His saintly virtues, his devout hospitality, his Benedictine wisdom in matters relating to wine and the success of his evangelical mission to spread the word throughout the world, earned him the title of the 'pape du vin' (Pope of Wine) from a New York journalist who once heard his confession. When Alexis Lichine bought le Prieuré, a Cantenac *4ᵉ cru classé*,

Alexis Lichine, the Pope of Wine, in his garden at Prieuré.

in 1951, it consisted of 11 hectares of ailing vines, run-down *chais* and a house that was sorely in need of repair. His success against such odds is remarkable, controversial and admirable.

Remarkable because in the short space of thirty years he has restored the long-lost reputation of Château Prieuré. The vineyard has been rebuilt from scratch. Initially Lichine exchanged some plots of land with the neighbouring properties, most notably with Emmanuel Cruse, who was also at this time restoring the Issan property. Later he purchased piece after piece of land, sometimes only tiny patches. He also bought many farms in the best possible areas. The *chais* were restored bit by bit, as were the vat houses and other production buildings. During this period, the good Alexis established a snug country seat and made this the centrepiece of his operations, installing all his antique furniture as well as several paintings by contemporary masters, including the finest Fontanarosa I have ever seen. In order that the foreign press photographers could shoot the full story, he brought home a St Bernard called Bacchus and a collie called Margaux.

Controversial because Alexis Lichine's advertising methods have been, right from the beginning, a violent break with the previous understatement of the Bordeaux and

Médoc establishment. With his innate sense of the dramatic and pronounced theatrical nature, he had directed a drama in a hundred acts, written as he went along and enacted in his drawing and dining rooms. By the roadside and on every wall, huge freshly painted placards proclaim the rebirth of the Prieuré-Lichine vineyards throughout the Médoc. This is typical of the extrovert, all things to all men.

The work accomplished by this exceptional man is certainly admirable. If one might sometimes complain that one finds the man himself rather too imposing, it is, nevertheless, impossible to deny the outstanding nature of his work. He united an army of importers, distributors, restaurateurs and wine-lovers from all over the Bordeaux area. Most of this was to his own advantage but, of course, everyone benefited in the long run.

From 1950 to 1970 Lichine widely publicized French wines and those of Bordeaux, with special emphasis on the Mêdoc and Margaux. With 60 hectares of vines throughout the whole appellation area and spacious, ultra-modern *chais*, Château Prieuré-Lichine is now one of the foremost Margaux varieties, far in excess of its official *4ᵉ cru* classification. The variety of its lands perfectly complements the variety of grape production. Some of the vines are a little lacking in maturity but, on the whole, Château Prieuré-Lichine has reached a standard that is well able, from year to year, to equal the very best of Margaux wines.

Quatre Vents (Clos des)

cru artisan

Main area: Soussans **Owner:** René Renaud, who oversees both direction and production **Surface area of vineyard:** 3 hectares (total property 12 hectares) **Average age of vines:** 20 years **Grape production:** Traditional **Production:** 12,000 bottles **Local sales:** Tel (56) 88 30 87, **and by mail order** (France only): Clos des Quatres Vents, Bourriche, Soussans, 33460 Margaux **Retail sales**

Here we have a château which has weathered all storms: René Renaud is the great-grandson of a wine-grower, a Soussanais of old stock. Part of his tiny 3 hectare vineyard runs almost into the town itself, and seems to serve as a sundial marked by the shadow of the church tower. The other part is in Marsac, on the best gravelly Soussans soil, at the end of the Margaux commune.

René Renaud has a fine palate, an indispensable quality for a good wine-grower. Growing the grapes is one thing, harvesting and pressing them is another, as is choosing the exact moment for bottling. This talent for choosing the right moment to move from one stage of production to the next is vital to the success of the vintage. It is by tasting rather than by chemical analysis that one knows when to rack the wine.

The Clos des Quatre Vents and René Renaud produce a strongly scented wine,

There is a distinctly British influence in the profile of Rausan-Ségla.

clearly coloured and surprisingly smooth to the taste. What is also surprising is its price, one of the most modest of the Margaux appellation.

Rambaud (Château)

Main area: Soussans **Owner:** André Fort, who oversees both direction and production, Tel (56) 88 32 62 **Surface area of vineyard:** 1.45 hectares **Average age of vines:** 40 years **Grape production:** Traditional **Production:** 5000 bottles **Retail sales:** Through Bordeaux shippers

cru artisan

Rausan-Ségla (Château)

2e cru classé

Main area: Margaux **Owner:** Holt Frères et Fils **President:** Jacques Théo **Director:** René Baffert **Steward:** Michel Bruzaud **Surface area of vineyard:** 43 hectares (total property 66 hectares) **Average age of vines:** 23 years **Grape production:** 66% Cabernet-Sauvignon, 28% Merlot, 4% Cabernet-Franc, 2% Petit-Verdot **Production:** 168,000–192,000 bottles **Local sales:** Tel (56) 88 70 30, **and by mail order** (France only): At the above address **Retail sales:** Louis Eschenauer SA, Tel (56) 81 58 90

For centuries Rausan wine has held pride of place among the Médoc *2ᵉ crus*. The 1855 classification bestowed this distinction on both Rausan-Ségla and Rauzan-Gassies, placing them immediately after Mouton (the distinction between Rausan with an 's' and Rauzan with a 'z' dates from the end of the nineteenth century). It was the Revolution which broke up the partnership between the two Rausans and, considering this period of time as far as wine production is concerned, one sees that there were a number of major upheavals in the Margaux region. At the beginning of the sixteenth century the noble house of Gassies was extremely prominent; both Gaillard de Tardes and Bernard de Faverolles were owners of the property. In 1661, however, the rich merchant Pierre des Mesures de Rausan bought the lands as well as those of Château Margaux and, a little later, Château Latour. As for the alternative spellings of Rausan, different authors have disagreed as to the exact history of the varieties. It seems safe to assume that Pierre des Mesures de Rausan was in full possession, at the end of the seventeenth century, of an important number of vineyards. In 1775, however, the purchase of the Gassies (or Garcies) took place and is attributed to another M. de Rausan, a councillor in the Bordeaux parliament. It is now apparent that the property had, over the span of two centuries, been divided and reunited several times. The last Rausan descendant, Baroness Castelpers, sold Rausan-Ségla in 1866 to the Senator Eugène Durand-Dassié. He passed on the property to his son-in-law, Frédéric Cruse. M. de Melson was the owner between 1956 and 1960, until the naval defence company, John Holt of Liverpool, became owner, having taken over Louis Eschenauer's company in Bordeaux.

As previously mentioned, the classification of 1855 placed the two Rausan wines at the head of *2ᵉ cru*, just after Mouton. This classification was the crowning glory of a wine already well known among connoisseurs: 'I would never buy Château Margaux because it is too expensive, but its neighbour, Rausan, is much better value.' This popularity was extremely pronounced in England, where M. de Rausan (or Rauzan?) carefully kept up his publicity campaign. Towards the middle of the eighteenth century, having grown impatient to sell a harvest which he thought particularly exceptional, he had it loaded on to a merchant ship and accompanied it in person to London. On board this floating *chai*, near the famous Tower of London, he extolled the virtues of his wine to the assembled society of London. This was extremely successful both in the press and by word of mouth in the salons of Kensington and St James's. But M. Rausan's expectations were so high that he was extremely disappointed with the level of bidding for his wine. Choosing his moment, however, he ordered the sailors to throw a barrel into the Thames to indicate that the prices proposed were not high enough. Like a street vendor smashing a pile of plates on the pavement because no one wants to buy, he followed the first barrel with a second, and then a third, each time raising the selling price of the remainder in proportion to the loss. As the fourth barrel hit the water, hands were raised to bid on the quayside, and he finally got the price he wanted.

The Rausan-Ségla wine is one of the finest of the Margaux appellation. The poor soil makes it rather thin, but nonetheless it has a rare elegance. During the colder, damper years it has little success. At those times, as Tristan Bernard commented, talking of coffee: 'Its goodness inclines towards weakness.' One must be a great lover of delicacy and subtlety to appreciate the quiet qualities of Rausan-Ségla. It is a perfect wine for candlelit dinner parties of exquisite dishes shared between good friends. It is often said that Margaux wines have truly feminine qualities and Rausan-Ségla epitomizes them.

Rausan under the ownership of Senator Durand-Dassié.

Rauzan-Gassies (Château)

2ᵉ cru classé

Main area: Margaux **Owner:** SCI de Château Rauzan-Gassies **Director:** Mme Paul Quié and J.-M. Quié **Chef de culture:** Marc Espagnet **Maître de chai:** Jean-Marc Espagnet **Surface area of vineyard:** 30 hectares (total property 30 hectares) **Average age of vines:** 25–30 years **Grape production:** 40% Cabernet-Sauvignon, 39% Merlot, 20% Cabernet-Franc, 1% Petit-Verdot **Production:** 100,000 bottles **Local sales:** Tel (56) 71 88 71, or in Paris, Tel (1) 368 08 41, **and by mail order:** Château Rauzan-Gassies, 33460 Margaux, or SCI Rauzan-Gassies, 135 rue de Paris, 94220 Charenton **Retail sales:** Several of the large Bordeaux shippers

Rauzan-Gassies was separated from the greater Rausan property towards the end of the eighteenth century. The vineyard consists of several small separate plots of land which, taken together, constitute a fair cross-section of the different varieties of soil found in the Margaux area. There are deep gravelly beds and sandy areas with clayey or ferruginous subsoil. Some of the vines are right in the heart of the village of Margaux. The 'château' is, in fact, a collection of production buildings, right next to Château Rausan-Ségla. Coming from Bordeaux and arriving at the sign announcing entry to Margaux, one cannot help but notice the two Rausan properties to the left beside Dufort.

Paul Quié bought Rauzan-Gassies in 1943. His wife and son, Jean-Michel, are now in charge of the vineyard, aided by Espagnet and his son. After a small dip in popularity, this variety has now come back to full strength and is sold as an equal to Rausan-Ségla, Brane and Lascombes. Although the majority of the better vineyards in Margaux have been completely rearranged since 1855, Rauzan-Gassies has remained more or less unchanged. One can easily trace the beneficial influence of M. Rhoné-Pereire, 173 owner at the end of the nineteenth century. The wine's great reputation really dates, however, from the time of M. de Rauzan (see Rausan-Ségla). It is said that in the space of twenty years he turned this property into a model vineyard through his exceptional wine-making skills. His success was so outstanding that the other wine-growers in the area suspected him of witchcraft. The villagers crossed themselves when he walked by and his workmen hid millet in their trouser bottoms. Suspicions grew when one year the surrounding vineyards suffered from frost and Rauzan remained untouched. The crunch came when a tremendous hail storm hit the neighbouring vineyards several days before the harvest. The cutters and porters became alarmed and refused to bring in the Rauzan harvest. Sensing the danger, M. de Rauzan called together every last one of the Margaux residents and protested his innocence: 'You believe I am a sorcerer and it is totally untrue!' An old man challenged him: 'M. de Rauzan, it is well known that you are a freemason.' 'Yes, that is true, but only as far as good sense is concerned. There in nothing supernatural in that – in fact, to the contrary, it is extremely natural. I'm going to let you in on my great secret.' The peasants became silent with anticipation. 'You believe that I have made a contract with the devil and that his demons work in my vineyards at night . . . also that there have been huge black birds using their wings to protect the crops from frost and hailstones. All of this is mere hearsay and superstition. My secret is very simple: when I bought this vineyard, it was stocked with bad vines. I went to M. d'Argicourt, the owner of Château Margaux, and asked him for some good plants to stock my fields. This good neighbour helped me tremendously both practically and through the best advice. I have cultivated my vines exactly as they do at Château Margaux and because of that have achieved results almost as good as theirs. That is my only secret. If you all follow that plan the vineyards of Margaux will produce the best wines in the world.' Since that day, all the smallholders of the commune have become sorcerers in their own way. In remembrance of the miracles which protected the Rauzan-Gassies vines, the wine label is decorated with two magic wings.

The Rauzan-Gassies wine is distinctly different from its neighbour Rausan-Ségla. It is much more full-bodied because of its strong constitution, and rather lacking in finesse. Sometimes one can detect a particular taste, unique to the property and surprisingly strong. With age this is transformed into a heady bouquet. It is much more aggressive than the other Margaux wines and has a strong personality which one either loves or hates. In comparison with my remarks on Rausan-Ségla, it seems to me that it is Rauzan-Gassies who wears the trousers in these two households . . . but sometimes these are of velvet or silk.

Saint-Marc (Château)

Main area: Soussans **Owner:** Marc Faure, who oversees both direction and production **Surface area of vineyard:** 7 hectares (total property 15 hectares) **Average age of vines:** 25 years **Grape production:** Malbecs, Cabernets, Merlots and Verdots **Production:** 20,000 bottles **Local sales:** Tel (56) 88 30 67, **and by mail order:** Château Saint-Marc, Soussans, 33460 Margaux **Retail sales**

Marc Faure has owned the Saint-Marc vineyard since 1958. The largest part of the property has been passed down through his family for generations, but over the last twenty years he has purchased several new pieces of land, increasing the area to 7 hectares, a sizeable property in the Margaux appellation. The grape growing and wine making are carried out in the most traditional fashion.

The wines have a peculiar character in that they cover a wide range of distinctive tastes, caused by the diversity of the soil in which the grapes are produced: gravel, clayey gravel, chalky clay and siliceous. Their long fermentation makes them rich in tannin and, as a result, rather lacking in smoothness but with increased strength and body. They improve through ageing for several years after bottling.

Siran (Château)

cru remarquable

Main area: Labarde **Owner:** William-Alain B. Miailhe, assisted by J. Daney **Surface area of vineyard:** 35 hectares (total property 95 hectares) **Average age of vines:** 38 years **Grape production:** Red: 50% Cabernet-Sauvignon, 25% Merlot, 15% Verdot, 10% Cabernet-Franc **Production:** 150,000 bottles **Local sales:** Tel (56) 88 34 04, or in Bordeaux, Tel (56) 81 35 01, **and by mail order:** 6 quai Louis-XVIII, BP 35, 33024 Bordeaux Cedex **Retail sales:** 'Occasionally'

Like the neighbouring Dauzac property, Siran was dependent on the refuge of Saint-Croix, which extended across the parishes of Macau and Labarde. Guilhem de Siran was a staunch supporter of Saint-Croix in the fifteenth century. Along with many of the Médoc properties, Siran went through a difficult time during the Revolution. The Count of La Roque Bouillac, who was then owner, emigrated in 1791. His daughter Jeanne united the property by marrying Alphonse, Count of Toulouse-Lautrec. Their son, Henri, was the well-known painter.

Siran was unluckily left unclassified in 1855, although its standing was high during the eighteenth century and a classification in 1848 refers to a vintage known as Bellegarde among the 4e *crus*. This was at the time the property of the celebrated Count J.-B. Lynch, and Bellegarde is in fact the name of the flat area of gravelly soil in Labarde, which is now part of the Siran property. M. Léo Barbier bought Château Siran in 1848. For almost two centuries the Barbier-Miailhe families, originally from Portets in the Gironde, had been renowned wine-brokers. William-Alain B. Miailhe is the latest descendant of this line and his avowed ambition is to have Siran rated as 175

The facilities at Château Siran are in no way inferior to those of the grands crus classés.

a *cru classé*. Perhaps this will one day be the case but, whatever the outcome, he has cultivated a fine property which is well known for its efficiency and professionalism. All the production buildings are painted pink and there are several other surprises on the estate including a heliport, constructed on the roof terrace of the *chais* beside huge reception rooms. There is also a small tower lined with cabinets full of Oriental china from the eleventh to the fifteenth centuries. Finally there is an old nuclear shelter converted into a wine cellar with an armoured door bearing the inscription: 'Better red than dead'. Alain Miailhe is a great historian and collector. He has assembled about him a multitude of objects related to wine and wine-growing and also has a fine

reproduction of the agricultural survey made of the Margaux area in 1828, compiled by a team from Bordeaux University, directed by Professor Pijassou. This will no doubt be of great use when a new classification is finally considered . . .

Following the example of Philippe de Rothschild, Alain Miailhe has had wine labels designed by contemporary artists. In 1980, the engraver Decaris chose to commemorate the events in Gdansk. In 1981, Folon celebrated the conquest of space by the shuttle Columbia. In 1982, Joán Miró designed a label for the World Cup Football tournament. This obviously does not improve the wine, but it is symbolic of the efforts of its present-day owner to record the feats of human endeavour over the

Whereas the waterside properties once had a port, Siran now has its own heliport.

years. Professor Emile Peynaud visits Siran from time to time to test the development of the latest vintages. It is generally recognized that, during the last few years, Château Siran has had its share of success. The wines are usually full-bodied, rich in bouquet and smooth to the palate. They are in no way as distinguished as the wines of Margaux and Cantenac, but are sometimes preferable for their honest qualities to the thinner vintages of the great masters.

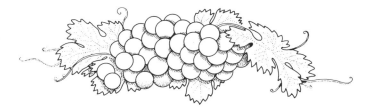

Tayac (Château)

cru bourgeois

Main area: Soussans **Owner:** A. Favin **Steward:** Mme Portet **Surface area of vineyard:** 34 hectares (total property 55 hectares) **Average age of vines:** 18 years **Grape production:** Red: 70% Cabernet-Sauvignon and Cabernet-Franc, 25% Merlot, 5% Petit-Verdot **Production:** 200,000 bottles **Local sales:** Tel (56) 88 33 06, **and by mail order** (in France and abroad): M. Favin, Tayac, Soussans, 33460 Margaux **Retail sales:** Savour Club, Maison Ginestet, Maison Quancard, Maison Lebègue

André Favin inherited Château Tayac in 1960. With 34 hectares of vineyard, it is both one of the largest of the smaller properties and one of the smallest of the larger. It has an important position on a flat area around the village of Tayac in the Soussans commune in the extreme north-west of the Margaux appellation area. Here the soil is sandy with chalky clay subsoil. At the beginning of the century, Château Tayac only covered an area of 18 hectares and Féret rated it as being among the *'crus bourgeois* and *1er artisans'*, at the same time drawing attention to the fact that the vineyard would respond well if extended. At this time, Margaux was not in itself an appellation area, and the Tayac property bordered on Avensan and Moulis. Producing wines grown in the richer palus soil did nothing to improve the variety's reputation. A new piece of land was added after the division of Château Haut-Breton Lariguadière, a *cru bourgeois supérieur*; and at the end of the nineteenth century the wine-making at Tayac was supervised by M. Mellet, owner of the Dubignon-Talbot property. In 1892, the estate was divided and only recently united by the Favin family.

André Favin is an accomplished wine-grower who absorbed his viticultural knowledge through a kind of natural osmosis. He is an expert in all stages of production, from planting to tasting. He is also a building contractor and, under this title, has been responsible for the construction or enlargement of many of the *chais* in the Margaux

André Favin among his produce.

179

area, most notably on the Prieuré-Lichine property. He has greatly modernized his property, making it much more functional and yet still pleasant for visitors. The wines he produces are a good reflection of his character, being robust and jovial with natural delicate finesse.

Tayac-Plaisance (Château)

Main area: Soussans **Owner:** Paul Bajeux, who oversees both direction and production **Surface area of vineyard:** 1.2 hectares **Average age of vines:** 30 years **Grape production:** 800 square metres of Merlot, 250 square metres of Cabernet-Sauvignons, 1500 square metres of Cabernet-Francs and Petits-Verdots **Production:** 5000–7000 bottles

Tayac-Plaisance is the hobby which employs Paul Bajeux's time when he is not working in his masonry business. This small vineyard belongs to his family and the Petit-Verdot vines are some of the oldest in the Soussans commune. Strictly limited in quantity, Paul Bajeux's production is worthy of its position among the better *crus artisans* in the Margaux appellation.

Tertre (Château du)

8ᵉ cru classé

Main area: Arsac **Owner:** Société du Château du Tertre **Administrator:** Philippe Gasqueton **Surface area of vineyard:** 48 hectares (total property 80 hectares) **Average age of vines:** 25 years **Grape production:** Red **Production:** 180,000 bottles

The gravelly soil beds of Château du Tertre rise to a height of 24 metres above sea level in the Arsac commune, and are the highest point in the Margaux appellation. The subsoil is chalky and ferruginous, which gives the Tertre wines a peculiar character, similar to that of the Graves in Bordeaux.

When Thomas, the brother of Michel de Montaigne, married Jacquette d'Arsac, he became owner of a large piece of land in the Médoc. He also had property on the coast, to the south of Soulac, near Négade headland at Lilhan. These lands, however, were gradually eroded by the Atlantic and covered by the sand dunes built up by the sea: 'In the Médoc along the shore, my brother the lord of Arsac, saw his lands disappear beneath the sand the sea cast before it,' wrote Montaigne to La Boétie. The two brothers and their friends got together at Château La Tour Carnet at Saint-Laurent, which was the home of their sister Madeleine, the wife of Thibaut de Camin. The Ségur family were already in possession of the Tertre property as far back as the eighteenth century. It was then united with the Château d'Arsac as one large property until the Revolution. Later it passed through the hands of various owners such as Brézet, Henry, Vallandé, Koenigswarter and Bernheim. During the 1930s and Second

The hilly vineyards of Château du Tertre.

World War the Château's fortunes declined. Philippe Capbern-Gasqueton, who also owns Calon-Ségur in Sainte-Estèphe, is the present-day administrator of the Société civile du Château du Tertre and its 50 hectares of vineyards. Château du Tertre is the only *cru classé* in the Arsac commune and shares, along with Dauzac, a fifth rating in the Margaux appellation. The château is in the process of being restored and the vineyard is now in good condition. All that remains is for this excellent variety to gain the recognition it deserves.

Treilles (Domaine des)

cru artisan

Main area: Soussans **Owner:** Guy Nouaux, who oversees both direction and production **Surface area of vineyard:** 3500 square metres (total property 6000 square metres) **Average age of vines:** 40 years **Grape production:** Malbec, Cabernet and Merlot **Production:** 1800 bottles **Local sales:** Tel (56) 88 31 54, **and by mail order:** Domaine des Treilles, 1 rue Montaigne, 33460 Margaux **Retail sales:** Ets Marcellin Marceau, Bordeaux

---

Guy Nouaux is owner of some of the oldest vines in Arsac, as is fitting since his family is also one of the oldest in the area. The whole vineyard is run in a traditional style, including the replacement of vine stalks only when the original vine is completely dead. The vines are also kept extremely short and it was not long ago that the vineyard was worked by horses.

The wine is fermented by infusing the grape skins in their juice and the product is a kind of 'bull's blood', that is to say an extremely tannic wine with very strong taste. The barrels are not often replaced but this is unimportant since the wine gets its

181

distinctive personality from this and, of course, the slightly acidic composition is extremely good for people suffering from sinusitis, pleurisy and gout. I heartily recommend a drop of this invigorating wine.

Trois Chardons (Château des)

cru artisan

Main area: Cantenac **Owners:** Claude, Yves and Pierre Chardon, who oversee both direction and production **Surface area of vineyard:** 2.2 hectares (total property 2.6 hectares) **Average age of vines:** 30 years **Grape production:** Cabernet, Merlot, Petit-Verdot **Production:** 8000 bottles **Local sales:** Tel (56) 88 33 94, **and by mail order:** M. Chardon, Issan, Cantenac, 33460 Margaux

This property belongs to Pierre Chardon and his two sons, Claude and Yves. All three are big, rugged men, totally dedicated to their vineyard. Their main business is the direction of Château Palmer, which their family has run for many years (the grandsons Eric and Philippe are already working in the *chais* and the vineyards). They also spend a great deal of time doing public service. Pierre Chardon, who was born at Château Palmer, is honorary mayor of Cantenac, having overseen the commune for thirty-three years. His son, Claude, is deputy mayor. At weekends they gather together in this small vineyard which was once known as 'Grand-Caneyron'. At harvest time all the family, friends and neighbours come to lend a hand and have a good time together.

The wine from Château des Trois Chardons is extremely rare because so little is produced. It is one of the best made *crus artisans* in Margaux. Refined, elegant, feminine and highly perfumed, this wine is produced on a vineyard the size of a handkerchief. Which reminds one of the old story of the Bordeaux at court who, finding the bouquet of a particular wine extremely pleasant, declared 'it should be used to scent handkerchiefs.' Unfortunately, however, even sold in aerosols, there wouldn't be enough for everyone.

Vallière (Château)

cru artisan

Main area: Soussans **Owner:** J.-P. Touya, who oversees both direction and production **Surface area of vineyard:** 3500 square metres (total property 3500 square meters) **Average age of vines:** 11 years **Grape production:** Traditional **Production:** 1200 bottles **Local sales:** M. J.-P. Touya, Virefougasse, 33460 Soussans, Tel (56) 88 71 24

The small Château Vallière property, next to Virefougasse, is cultivated by Jean-Pierre Touya in his spare time. The wine label is typical of the old-fashioned kind produced by Bordeaux printers. They originally made up a catalogue which presented pictur-

esque scenes from the vineyards of the Gironde. The wine-grower could choose between 20 harvest scenes, 12 scenes of men at work, 14 pretty girls at the harvest, 140 views of the various châteaux and all the best-known methods of transporting wine, on foot, by horse, by carriage and sailing ship. Wetterwald printing factory, founded in 1815, was the first to produce the Bordeaux wine labels, printed in photogravure or lithography. The Château Vallière label carries the reference number 224 of the Wetterwald catalogue.

The wine has become almost a collector's item, like an extremely limited edition, since Jean-Pierre Touya harvests approximately one *tonneau* per year. This is roughly equivalent to four Bordeaux barrels or 1200 bottles. People I have spoken to who have been lucky enough to taste the wine tell me that they had no complaints.

Vieux Cep (Cru du)

The 10 ares and 26 centiares which constitute the Cru du Vieux Cep property were purchased in 1983 by Jean Joyeux, now in retirement in Margaux having been the third-generation steward in his family of Château Rausan-Ségla. This property was planted by his grand-  father and the vines are now older than him. The label no longer exists but I have included it in hommage to all the other varieties which disappeared over the generations and the centuries. An enormous amount of *crus bourgeois, artisans* and *paysans* have been absorbed by the more important properties. Sometimes their labels still exist as the name of the second wine produced by a *cru classé,* but more often they have disappeared. From time to time they resurface in the catalogue of the large auction houses, when an old-established wine cellar is put under the hammer. The châteaux, which were often fine, large houses at the end of the nineteenth century, have become strictly residential properties. Within the small area of the Margaux commune one can name among those varieties which have disappeared: Abel-Laurent, Doumens, Lamouroux, Lestonnat, La Tour de l'Aubion, La Gombeaude, La Colonilla, Richet-Marian.

Vincent (Château)

cru bourgeois supérieur

Main area: Cantenac **Owner** Mme Jean Domec; production is overseen by La Société du Château Palmer **Surface area of vineyard:** 5 hectares (total property 7 hectares) **Average age of vines:** 25 years **Grape production:** Traditional **Production:** 15,000 bottles **Local sales:** Tel (56) 88 30 12, **and by mail order** (in France and abroad): Château Vincent, Cantenac, 33460, Margaux

Château Vincent, the home of a great little wine.

I have already mentioned the Jadouin family as being important owners in the Margaux appellation and, more particularly, in Cantenac and Arsac. One of Jules Jadouin's daughters married a Lebègue, the other a Boiteau. The daughter of the Boiteau couple was subsequently married to Adolphe Domec, a master artist in glass in Bordeaux. In the eighteenth century, the old skills were well represented in the Bacalan area of Bordeaux by the Vieillard pottery and Domec glassworks.

Château Vincent is one of the prettiest little houses in the countryside, with its priest's garden and chapter-house. Mme Jean Domec is glad to leave Paris (where she has an up-and-coming antique shop selling items from the Edwardian era, at 40 rue Mazarine) to spend short breaks at Vincent, which is situated between Montbrun and Palmer. It is, indeed, Château Palmer which cultivates the 5 hectares of vineyards belonging to the property. The farm work is paid for in kind and after the vinification process is completed, carefully tended by the Chardon family, the wine is then aged in barrels in *chais* at Château Vincent, where it is ultimately bottled. Martine Domec has no lack of friends or relations to sample and buy up her produce. You can always try to break into this close circle, and you will certainly receive a warm welcome at Château Vincent.

Other known producers in the Margaux appellation area

	Surface area of vineyard	Average age of vines	Grape production
Bordes, Marie	62 ares	30 years	Merlot
Delas, Marguerite	40 ares	24 years	Merlot Cabernet-Sauvignon, Petit-Verdot
Icard, Jeanne	37 ares	40 years	75% Merlot 25% Cabernet-Sauvignon
Meyre, Henri	32 ares	55 years	50% Merlot 50% Cabernet-Sauvignon
Rex, Roger	1.6 hectares	17 years	Traditional
Videau, Jeanne	6.57 ares	35 years	Merlot

Note: 1 are = 100 square metres

Appendices

A short guide to vintages of the Margaux appellation

Year	Hectares in production	Hectolitres produced	Average yield per hectare	Success of the vintage	Ageing
1955	656	18,148	27.65	●●●●○	■■
1956	609	7739	12.70	●○	
1957	570	7924	13.89	●●●	■■■■
1958	538	8627	16.02	●●○	■
1959	610	12,868	21.10	●●●○	■■■
1960	613	16,337	26.65	●●○	
1961	610	7257	11.90	●●●●●●	■■■■■■
1962	634	16,069	25.36	●●●○	■■
1963	676	23,461	34.68	●	
1964	715	28,585	40	●●○○	■
1965	724	21,817	30.14	○	
1966	757	22,197	29.33	●●●○	■■
1967	801	29,862	37.31	●●●●	■■■
1968	837	21,806	26.05	○	
1969	864	17,530	20.29	●●○	■
1970	908	35,492	39.06	●●●●○	■■■■
1971	899	19,675	21.88	●●●○	■■
1972	893	24,278	27.18	●○	
1973	912	38,474	42.20	●●●○	■■
1974	894	39,488	44.18	●●○	■
1975	936	27,173	29.03	●●●●●●	■■■■■■■
1976	988	37,674	38	●○○	■
1977	1050	21,849	21	●●	■■■
1978	1036	34,137	33	●●●○○	■■
1979	1052	49,373	47	●●●●	■■■■
1980	1052	34,048	32	●●○	■■
1981	1065	43,300	40.65	●●●○	■■■■
1982	1101	60,770	55	●●●●○	■■■■■
1983	1146	58,372	50	●●●●●	■■■■■■

Notes

Some of the varieties suffered from hailstorms. A few remarkable successes.

One can still find good examples of this year.

This wine is rather acidic and tends to get worse with age.

Several vintages are very good, in particular Palmer.

The quality is below standard.

Château Margaux is incredible. Good drinking wines.

A 'vintage of the century'.

A good year with just a trace of acidity.

Two or three are worthy of note.

Rather irregular in quality, with some successes and some disappointments.

Not worth speaking of.

In my opinion, nowadays better than the '67 vintage.

Full-bodied wines, but a little hard.

None available.

Sometimes disappointing.

A good year which will age well.

Much better than their reputation would have one believe; very good for immediate drinking.

Best drunk young.

An average year; some agreeable wines.

Some successes in an otherwise unremarkable vintage.

Still rather young, they are in no way as good as the '61 vintage but it is a shame to drink them yet.

Nothing to be gained by ageing; an average year.

Strong in acidity and mainly disappointing.

A good year for very smooth wines, ready to drink now.

A very good year which is ageing well.

Rather light, they make good luncheon wines.

A good year which should improve.

A very good year which will go down in history.

The best year since '61; exceptionally good wines.

Comments

It is possible to trace on this table, over the last 30 years, the relationship between the surface area of vineyards and the yields obtained. It is thus possible to calculate the number of hectolitres produced against the number of hectares worked and to see that this is not always inversely proportional to the quality of the wine (for example: 11.9 hectolitres in 1961, 30.06 in 1970 and 50 in 1983).

The total number of circles in the central column indicates the degree of success of that particular vintage. The number of black circles indicates the liveliness of the wines. The ageing column shows the future of a vintage from the present time. Certain years are 'dead'. One rectangle corresponds to a period of three to five years. Thus a vintage with four rectangles could have an expected lifespan of twelve to twenty years.

Index of owners

Angludet (Sté civile Château d'	*Château d'Angludet*	97
Augeau, Pierre	*Château Ligondras*	138
Bajeux, Paul	*Château Tayac-Plaisance*	180
Barreau Roland	*Bouquet de Monbrison*	101
Bernaleau, Régis	*Château Mongravey*	157
Bordes, Marie		185
Bosc, Jacques	*Château de Les Graves du Sol*	138
Boutain, Jean-Marc	*Château de Pichecan*	164
Boyd-Cantenac et Pouget (GFA des Châteaux)	*Château Boyd-Cantenac* *Château Pouget*	101 166
Boyer, Pierre	*Château Bel Air-Marquis d'Aligre*	99
Brunet, Michel	*Château Les Baraillots*	137
Cantenac Brown (Société civile du Château)	*Cantenac Brown*	105
Chantovent (Sté) and Taillan (Sté)	*Château La Gurgue*	130
Chardon, Claude, Yves et Pierre	*Château des Trois Chardons*	182
Chateau, Bernard	*Château Larruau*	132
Chatellier et Fils (SAF)	*Château Dauzac*	109
Clauzel-Binaud (Indivision)	*Château La Tour-de-Mons*	136
Condom, Jean-Robert	*Château Labégorce*	126
Corporeau, A.	*Clos de L'Aiguillette*	131
Davis (Elizabeth and her sons)	*Château Monbrison*	155
Delas, Marguerite		185
Domec, Mme Jean	*Château Vincent*	184

Dufourg-Landry, M.	*Château des Graviers*	118
Dulos, Simone and J.-P. Seyat-Dulos	*Château Martinens*	153
Eyquem, Marcel	*Château Hautes-Graves*	120
Faure, Marc	*Château Saint-Marc*	175
Favin, A.	*Château Tayac*	179
Fort, André	*Château Rambaud*	170
Gassies, Louis	*Château Gassies du Vieux-Bourg*	115
Giscours (GFA du Château)	*Château Giscours*	115
Holt Frères et Fils	*Château Rausan-Ségla*	171
Icard, Jeanne		185
Issan (Sociét civile du Château d')	*Château d'Issan*	121
Labégorce Zédé (GFA)	*Château Labégorce-Zédé*	128
Lebègue et Cie SA (J.)	*Château Montbrun*	157
Lichine (SA)	*Château Ferrière*	114
	Château Lascombes	133
Lurton, Lucien	*Château Brane-Cantenac*	103
	Château Desmirail	111
	Château Durfort-Vivens	112
	Château La Tour de Bessan	135
Margaux (SCA Château)	*Château Margaux*	141
	Pavillon Blanc du Château Margaux	163
Marsac Séguineau (SC du Château)	*Château Marsac Séguineau*	152
Maugey, Albert	*Domaine La Rose Maucaillou*	131
Mestrie, André	*Clos de Bigos*	101
Meyre, Henri		185
Miailhe, William-Alain B.	*Château Siran*	175
Mondon (M. et Mme)	*Château Clos de La Gravière*	108
Mour, G. de	*Château Haut Breton Larigaudière*	119
Nouaux, Guy	*Domaine des Treilles*	181
Palmer (SCI Château)	*Château Palmer*	158

Paveil (GFA du Château)	*Château Paveil de Luze*	162
Pontac-Lynch (GFA du Château)	*Château Pontac-Lynch*	164
Poujeau, René	*Château Graveline*	118
Prieuré-Lichine (SA Château)	*Château Prieuré-Lichine*	167
Rabi, Georges	*Domaine de Maucaillou*	155
Rauzan-Gassies (SCI de Château)	*Château Rauzan-Gassies*	173
Raymond, Marc	*Cru de Castelbruck*	107
Renaud, René	*Clos des Quatre Vents*	169
Renon, René et Jeanne	*Château Charmant*	108
	Château La Galiane	129
Rex, Rodger		185
Rocher Cap-de-Rive (Vignobles)	*Château Pontet-Chappaz*	166
Rooryck (J. & S.)	*Château Canuet*	106
Saux, Christian et Viviane	*Château Haut-Tayac*	120
Schröder & Schÿler et Cie	*Château Kirwan*	124
Sénéclauze, Pierre-Louis, Philippe et Jean	*Château Marquis de Terme*	150
Seynat-Dulos, Jean-Pierre and Dulos, Simone	*Château Martinens*	153
Sorge, Jean	*Château Deyrem-Valentin*	112
Taillan (Sté Bernard) and Chantovent (Sté)	*Château La Gurgue*	130
Tertre (Sté du Château du)	*Château du Tertre*	180
Touya, J.-P.	*Château Vallière*	182
Videau, Jeanne		185
Zuger, Jean-Claude	*Château Marquis d'Alesme-Becker*	148
Zuger, Roger	*Château Malescot Saint-Exupéry*	139

Picture acknowledgements
Alain Danvers: 78, 84; Château Giscours – Aérovue Diffusion, Mérignac: 116; Luc Joubert, Paris: 20, 24, 37, 52, 73, 75, 76, 80, 142, 145; Château Labégorce-Zédé – Photo Thiépont: 129; Michel Plassart, Paris: 49; Château Siran: 176, 178; Château Vallière: 183. All the remaining pictures by Claude Lada and Douglas Metzler.